METAPHYSICS OF WAR

Metaphysics *of* War

Battle, Victory & Death *in the* World *of* Tradition

by
Julius Evola

Arktos
MMXI

Third English edition published in 2011 by Arktos Media Ltd.

First edition published in 2007 by Integral Tradition Publishing.

Second edition published in 2008 by Integral Tradition Publishing.

Printed in the United Kingdom

ISBN 978-1-907166-36-5

BIC classification: Social & political philosophy (HPS);
Theory of warfare and military science (JWA);
Philosophy of religion (HRAB)

Editor: John B. Morgan
Cover Design: Andreas Nilsson
Layout: Daniel Friberg

ARKTOS MEDIA LTD.

www.arktos.com

Contents

Introduction

by John B. Morgan IV

The Julius Evola to be found in this volume is one who has, thus
far, remained largely unknown to English-speaking readers,
apart from how he has been described second-hand by other
writers – namely, the political Julius Evola. With the exception
of *Men Among the Ruins*, which defines Evola's post-war political
attitude, as well as the essays made available on-line and in print
from the *Evola as He Is* Web site, all of Evola's works which have
been translated into English prior to the present volume have
been his works on esotericism, and this is the side of his work
with which English-language readers are most familiar. The essays
contained in this book were written during the period of Evola's
engagement with both Italian Fascism and German National
Socialism, and, while Evola regarded these writings as being only a
single aspect – and by no means an aspect of primary importance
– of his work, it is for these writings that he is most often called
to account (and nearly always harshly condemned) in the court
of the academicians and professional historians. For this reason
alone, then, it is of great value that these essays are being made
available so that English-speaking readers can now form their
own opinion of Evola's work in this area. And for those who are
interested in Evola as a teacher, then these essays will serve to
open up an area of his work that his hitherto remained largely

inaccessible, and which contains a great deal of practical advice for the traditionally-minded student.

It is important to remember while reading these essays, however, that Evola himself made no distinction between the various areas of culture with which he chose to engage – areas which have been artificially divided from each other by the philosophy of modernity, which treats the entire body of universal knowledge as a creature to be dissected and examined, one organ at a time, beneath a microscope, and thus each part of the creature's body is only understood as a thing in itself, without any understanding of how it relates to the whole. Evola's approach to knowledge was traditional, and therefore it was integrated in nature. For him, there was always only one subject: Tradition, which, as his friend René Guénon had first defined it, is the timeless and unchanging esoteric core which lies at the heart of all genuine spiritual paths. 'Traditionalism', a term which Evola himself never used, refers to the knowledge and techniques derived from sacred texts that the individual can use to orient himself in order to know Tradition, and in knowing it, thereby live all aspects of his life in accordance with it. Politics was only of interest to Evola in terms of how the pursuit of certain political goals could be of benefit toward the spiritual advancement of a traditionally-minded individual, and also in terms of how the distasteful business of politics might be able to bring modern societies closer into line with the values and structures to be found within the teachings of traditional thought.

During the 1930s, two political phenomena seemed to bear some hopeful possibilities for him in terms of how they might be utilised as vehicles for the restoration of something at least approximating a traditional society: Italian Fascism and German National Socialism (Nazism). At no point, however, was Evola a starry-eyed, fanatical revolutionary, filled with idealistic enthusiasm for the cause. Indeed, in 1930 he wrote about Fascism, 'To the extent to which Fascism embraces and defends [traditional] ideals, we shall call ourselves Fascists. And this is all.'[1] Reflecting on his political engagements later in life, he further wrote:

---

1   Quoted by Evola himself in *The Path of Cinnabar* (London: Arktos, 2009), p. 106.

Philosophy, art, politics, science, even religion" were here stripped of any right and possibility to exist merely in themselves, and to be of any relevance outside a higher framework. This higher framework coincided with the very idea of Tradition... [My goal was] "to defend ideals unaffected by any political regime – be it Fascist, Communist, anarchist or democratic. These ideals transcend the political sphere; yet, when translated on the political level, they necessarily lead to qualitative differences – which is to say: to hierarchy, authority and *imperium* in the broader sense of the word" as opposed to "all forms of democratic and egalitarian turmoil.[2]

Taking all of Evola's comments into account, both before and after the war, he never considered himself to be very much of a Fascist. He understood from the beginning that both Fascism and National Socialism were thoroughly modern in their conception. In 1925, Evola had already written that Italian Fascism lacked a 'cultural and spiritual root', which it had only tried to develop after gaining power, 'just as a newly rich man later tries to buy himself an education and a noble title'.[3] He attacked the notions of patriotism that Fascism tried to inculcate into Italian society as mere 'sentimentality'. He also condemned the violence which Mussolini was using against his political opponents. He labelled the Fascist revolution as an 'ironic revolution',[4] which left far too much of the pre-existing political order untouched (a sentiment apparently shared by Hitler, who reputedly referred to Italian Fascism, with its odd blending of the dictatorial position of 'Il Duce' with the Fascist Grand Council and the traditional monarchy, as a 'half-job'). In later years he was to observe that, 'In strictly cultural terms, however, the Fascist "revolution" was simply a joke.'[5] Both

2 *Ibid.*, p. 106.
3 Quoted in H. T. Hansen's Introduction to Julius Evola, *Men Among the Ruins* (Rochester: Inner Traditions, 2002), p. 36.
4 *Ibid.*, p. 36.
5 *The Path of Cinnabar*, p. 114.

Fascism and National Socialism relied on the masses for their support, which set them apart from the rule by aristocracy of the traditional world, and National Socialism was obsessed by a race theory derived from modern, scientific concepts of evolution and biology which were thoroughly anti-traditional.

Given so many problems with Fascism and Nazism from a traditional perspective, then why did Evola ever show any interest in them at all? The answer lies in the spirit of the times. By the 1930s, it was clear that the democratic nations of Western Europe and the United States, the Communist Soviet Union, and the fascistic countries were all on a collision course with each other. And, despite their many flaws, the fascist movements, unlike democratic and Communist societies, were at least attempting to restore something akin to the traditional, hierarchical order within the social structure of the modern world – an order which had gone unquestioned throughout the histories of all civilisations for thousands of years, prior to the onset of modernity. While Fascism and National Socialism were thoroughly modernist in their conception, Evola believed that, given time, they could potentially be used as a gateway to re-establish an order in Europe based on genuinely traditional values, and that they might even eventually give rise to genuinely traditional social forms which would supercede them. It is in this context that these essays – some of which contain direct references to Fascism, being addressed to either Italian or German readerships as they originally were – should be understood.

Evola's political ideal was always the Roman Empire. It is invoked repeatedly throughout these essays. The Fascists spoke frequently about ancient Rome, just as the Nazis constantly invoked the myth of an idealised Nordic past. Their understanding of these ancient wonders, however, was of an extremely superficial sort, which in practice didn't extend beyond constructing new buildings in the style of the ancient world, and engendering artistic styles that were a mere imitation of the Classical era. Evola wanted to bring about change on a much deeper level. He didn't just want a few cosmetic changes to be made – he wanted modern-day Italians to actually resume thinking and behaving as their ancient ancestors had done. In short, he wanted the Italians to *become* like the ancient Romans – in thought, word and deed. This is why, for him, Fascism fell far short of his hopes for it – in his writings, he sometimes referred to what he wanted as 'super-fascism'. By using this term, he did not mean that he wished for more of what Fascism was already offering. Rather, he was calling for a *transcendence* of Fascism. He wanted for the Fascist revolution to tunnel inward, into the very soul of each individual Italian, and awaken the long-buried racial memory of their illustrious Imperial ancestors. When Italy disappointed him, he transferred his hopes to the Germans, particularly in the form of the *Schutzstaffel* (S.S.), which, with Heinrich Himmler's efforts to fashion it into something akin to a Medieval knightly order, seemed to hold a spark of the ancient Teutonic Knights within them. Evola was even invited to deliver a series of lectures to representatives of the S.S. leadership in 1938. However, the S.S. was fixated upon the Nazis' purely biological definitions of racial purity and their belief in the supremacy of the Nordic peoples, and as such they were unimpressed by the ideas of the 'Latin' Evola, who proposed the idea that spirit and character were as important to one's racial qualifications as ancestry and blood. He was politely sent away. As such, Evola's hope to influence the political forces of the period in such a way as to implement his plan for the spiritual and cultural regeneration of Europe was never to be realised.

The failure of Evola's efforts, however, should in no way be understood as reducing the relevancy of the essays in this volume to mere relics of purely historical interest. Evola's writing was always directed at the individual, and he believed that genuine change had to begin at that level before any meaningful political or social change could follow suit. Furthermore, the root of all of Evola's thinking lay in the unchanging world of Tradition. Therefore, the attitudes and orientations which he encouraged his readers to adopt as a way of preparing for the worldwide struggle of his time are just as relevant to a traditionally-minded individual preparing to steel himself for the struggles and conflicts of our own era, whether they are political or of an entirely different sort. The definitions of heroism and the qualities of the warrior that Evola describes herein are surely timeless and universal. Indeed, in 'Varieties of Heroism', one can easily see, in the phenomenon of today's Muslim 'suicide bombers', a supra-personal heroism of a type identical to that of the Japanese *kamikaze* pilots that Evola describes. While it would not be correct to label today's Islamist radicals as 'traditionalists', since their particular interpretation of Islam has modernist roots in the Nineteenth-century Salafi school, we can still see some elements of a traditional conception of the warrior in their actions. For instance, Evola describes at great length the concept of *jihad*, which, as he explains, involves an inner struggle against one's own weaknesses as well as the struggle against one's external enemies – those whose characteristics resemble those aspects of himself that the warrior is attempting to purge. Regrettably, this dual concept of *jihad* as consisting of an inward as well as an outward form of struggle has been rejected by today's Islamist radicals, who believe that the war against the infidels should take precedence over all other considerations. Fortunately, however, the dual understanding of *jihad* is still to be found among the Islamic mystics: the Sufis, who may very well be the last guardians of a traditional Islam in the modern world.

Despite these differences, however, an attack carried out by an Islamist 'suicide bomber' still retains the essential idea of self-sacrifice, and yearning for transcendence, that is to be found in the traditional warrior concept. In 'Varieties of Heroism', Evola explains why those Japanese *kamikaze* pilots who died while crashing their planes into American ships should not be regarded as suicides, since the pilots carried out these attacks with the belief that they were merely giving up this life in favour of a more transcendent and supra-personal existence. Given that Muslim 'suicide bombers' similarly believe that they are destined for Paradise as a result of their actions, the objection to such attacks on the basis of the *Qur'an*'s prohibition against suicide is, therefore, ludicrous. Such was, indeed, the motivation behind the famed

Ismaili Assassins of Alamut who terrorised the Islamic world, as well as the armies of the European Crusaders, for centuries. The Assassins carried out carefully-planned attacks on individual enemies without regard for the safety of the assassin, and, as such, the technique of the 'suicide attack' was their hallmark. The Assassins were always assured, however, that even if they were to die during the course of their attack, they would be rescued by angels, and sent to dwell in Paradise forever. Although the Assassins, who were a small offshoot of Shi'ism, are regarded as heretics by other Muslims, we can see the roots (or, perhaps, only a parallel) of today's 'suicide bombers' in their practices which is entirely consistent with Evola's description of the supra-personal mode of death in combat.

It is important for me to clarify that I am referring only to those attacks carried out against military or political targets. The mass-casualty attacks on civilians, which have become an all-too-common occurrence in Iraq and elsewhere in the Islamic world in recent years, are alien to the provisions of war laid out in traditional Islam, and can be justified only within the modern innovative doctrines of *takfir* – in which one can declare other Muslims to be apostates – or *jahiliyyah* – which regards fellow Muslims as living in a state of pagan ignorance. It is likewise forbidden in the *Qur'an* to attack the civilian population even of one's enemy, something which the Islamists have had to perform theological acrobatics to circumvent in order to justify their bloody attacks in the West. Certainly, such murderous behaviour, which is usually perpetrated out of desperation by individuals chosen from the lowest rungs of society, is not something which Evola would have defined as traditional or seen as desirable, even in opposition to societies he found detestable. Evola's ideal was that of the *kshatriya* described by Lord Krishna in the *Bhagavad-Gita*, which has been explained by A. C. Bhaktivedanta Swami Prabhupada as follows:

One who gives protection from harm is called *kshatriya*. ... The *kshatriyas* are specially trained for challenging and killing

because religious violence is sometimes a necessary factor.
... In the religious law books it is stated: 'In the battlefield,
a king or *kshatriya*, while fighting another king envious of
him, is eligible for achieving the heavenly planets after
death, as the brahmanas also attain the heavenly planets by
sacrificing animals in the sacrificial fire.' Therefore, killing
on the battlefield on religious principles and killing animals
in the sacrificial fire are not at all considered to be acts of
violence, because everyone is benefited by the religious
principles involved.[6]

A *kshatriya*, therefore, is not an ordinary man, but rather a man
of the highest aristocratic attitude and behavior. He does not
kill out of a desire to fulfil some selfish desire or to bring about
some temporary political gain. Rather, a *kshatriya* fights because
he knows that it is the reason for his existence, his *dharma*. He
fights to defend the principles of his religion and his community,
knowing that if he carries out his duty, regardless of victory or
defeat or even his own personal safety, he is destined to attain
the highest spiritual platform. But, unfortunately, few genuine
kshatriyas are to be found in the degenerate Kali-Yuga in which
we are now living.
    While Evola looked to the past for his understanding of the
genuine warrior, Evola was far ahead of his time in his understanding of politics, as were all of the 'Conservative Revolutionaries' in
Europe during the period between the wars who sought a form
of politics beyond the banal squabbles among parties that have
dominated in recent centuries. In our time, however, we find that
the ideas first outlined by Evola and others are finding new appeal
among those seeking an alternative to the seemingly unstoppable,
global spread of democratic capitalism. As more people grow
tired of the bland multicultural (or, more properly, anti-cultural)
consumer society that is being offered as a vision of utopia, it
seems likely that Evola's writings will only continue to increase

---

6   A. C. Bhaktivedanta Swami Prabhupada, *Bhagavad-Gita as It Is* (Mumbai:
    Bhaktivedanta Book Trust, 2008), Chapter 2, Text 31, p. 105.

in relevance as the cracks of social crisis continue to deepen. In particular, 'The Meaning of the Warrior Element for the New Europe' contains a number of insights which are just as relevant today as they were in 1941. In this essay, Evola discusses the First World War in the context of 'democratic imperialism', and the attempt by the Allies to put to an end the last vestiges of the traditional way of life that were embodied in the Central Powers. We see the exact same phenomenon at work today in the efforts of the United States to spread 'freedom' through military action in the Middle East and elsewhere, which is similarly designed to put an end to resistance in the last areas of the world which are still actively opposing the culture of materialism with traditional values. As such, we are now witnessing another case of 'democratic imperialism' by which the present-day democratic powers, having already succeeded in Europe, are attempting to destroy the last vestiges (and only a vestige, given how profoundly impacted by modernity the entire world has been over the last century) of the traditional conception of order. These forces will not be defeated through military means, however, but only by those who choose to embody the ideal of the warrior inwardly as well as outwardly, the world of Tradition being a realm which no amount of force or wealth can subdue.

This introduction will not contain a biographical summary of Evola's life, as that has already been done extensively by several writers elsewhere in the English language (most notable, particularly in terms of his political attitudes, is Dr. H. T. Hansen's Introduction to *Men Among the Ruins*), as well as in Evola's autobiography, *The Path of Cinnabar*. However, given that these essays are concerned primarily with war, it is worth mentioning that Evola did not understand war in a purely theoretical sense. Evola served as an artillery officer in the Italian army during the First World War, and he would have served again in the Second World War had not the controversial nature of his position in Fascist Italy intervened to prevent him from doing so. Evola practiced what he wrote. This is no more evident than in his essay 'Race and War', a passage from which seems like a premonition of the fate that was to befall him in 1945, when he was injured and paralysed for life from the waist down as the result of an air raid while he was working in Vienna. In it, Evola mentions a German article about bombing raids by aircraft, 'in which the test of sang-froid, the immediate, lucid reaction of the instinct of direction in opposition to brutal or confused impulse, cannot but result in a decisive discrimination of those who have the greatest prob-ability of escaping and surviving from those who do not'. Here we may, indeed, be catching a glimpse of the thinking behind his refusal to retreat to shelters during air raids, instead choosing to walk the streets as a test of his own fate.

Lastly, a word about where these essays originally appeared. In 1930, Evola established a bi-weekly journal of his own, *La Torre*, which was to focus on the critique of Fascism from a traditionalist perspective, written by Evola as well as other writers. His attacks on the failures of Fascism angered many in the Fascist establish-ment, however, and the authorities forced a halt to the publication of *La Torre* after only five issues. Evola therefore realised that, if he wanted to continue to attempt to reach an audience of those who might be sympathetic to his message of reform, he would need to find well-connected Fascist allies who would be willing to publish his writings, and he succeeded. This is the period to which nearly all of the essays in this book belong. Evola found an important ally in Giovanni Preziosi, who was the editor of the magazine, *La Vita Italiana* (see 'Varieties of Heroism'). Preziosi's publication was also sometimes critical of the Fascist regime, but Preziosi himself had earned Mussolini's trust and respect, and was thus allowed more freedom of content than most others. (According to Evola it was also rumoured that Preziosi possessed an archive of materials which, if made public, would embarrass many of the Fascist leaders.)[7] Preziosi had been an admirer of Evola's *La Torre,* and he was also a friend of Arturo Reghini, the great Italian esotericist who had been Evola's mentor and col-laborator when he first began studying spirituality and mysticism. He agreed to begin publishing Evola's writings in his own journal,

---

7   *The Path of Cinnabar*, p. 110.

and starting in 1936 he also funded many of Evola's trips to other countries, which he was making in an effort to build a network of contacts from among various 'Conservative Revolutionary' organisations all over Europe, in keeping with his hopes at the time of preparing a European – rather than a narrowly Italian – elite which might one day implement his 'super-Fascist' (or, as he himself put it, 'Ghibelline') ideals for the entire Continent. Evola himself wrote, 'My idea was that of coordinating the various elements which to some extent, in Europe, embodied traditionalist thought from a political and cultural perspective.'[8] This desire is quite evident within the pages of this book, as Evola constantly refers to Aryan civilisation, and cites references from the whole of European culture and history, rather than focusing exclusively on the Italian tradition, as most Fascist writers, with their more conventional sense of nationalism, were doing.

Preziosi also introduced Evola to Roberto Farinacci. Farinacci was a Fascist who had a personal relationship with Mussolini, and he was the chief editor of *Il Regime Fascista* (see the first six essays as well as 'The Roman Conception of Victory'), a journal which was an official publication of the Fascist Party. Farinacci was indifferent to Evola's past troubles with the regime, and he sought to elevate the cultural aspirations of the Fascist revolution. To this end, he granted Evola a page of his journal every other week, in which he was given *carte blanche* to write on whatever subject he wished. This page, which began to appear in 1933, was entitled 'Diorama Filosofico' (Philosophical Diorama), and it was subtitled 'Problems of the Spirit in Fascist Ethics'. Farinacci used his influence to deflect any attempt to rebuke Evola for writing about Fascism from a critical perspective. So it was that Evola was given an unassailable position from which to voice his observations. This situation was to continue for a full decade, until 1943. Frequently, Evola wrote the contents of the 'Diorama' himself, but he also used it as a forum to highlight like-minded thinkers, of both a literary as well as a political inclination, whom he wished to promote. Thus, by examining the history of Evola's efforts to

8   *The Path of Cinnabar*, p. 155.

publish politically-oriented texts during the Fascist era, we can understand the complexity of his relationship to Fascism in general, and thus see why it cannot be said with complete accuracy that Evola was either a Fascist or an anti-Fascist. The most truthful answer is that Evola saw in Fascism a possibility for something better, but that this possibility was one that remained unrealised.

For those newcomers to Evola who are seeking to understand the totality of his thought, these essays are not the ideal place to start. The foundation of all of his work is the book which was published shortly before the essays in this volume were written: *Revolt Against the Modern World*. This book lays out the metaphysical basis for all of his life's work, and one should familiarise himself with it before reading any of Evola's other writings. It should also be made clear that these essays were by no means Evola's last word on the subject of politics. Readers interested in where Evola's political thought ended up in the post-war years should consult his book *Men Among the Ruins*, in which he outlines his understanding of the concept of *apoliteia*, or the 'apolitical stance' which he felt was a necessary condition for those of a traditional inclination to adopt in the age of Kali-Yuga – the last, and most degenerate age within the cycle of ages as understood by in the Vedic tradition, and in which we are currently living. *Apoliteia* should not be confused with apathy or lack of engagement, however – it is, instead, a special form of engagement with political affairs that does not concern itself with the specific goals of politics, but rather with the impact of such engagement on the individual. This is not the place for an examination of this idea, however, as the essays in this book were written by a younger Evola, who felt that there was still a chance of restoring something of the traditional social order via the use of profane politics. Still, it is worth noting that in the very last essay in this volume, 'The Decline of Heroism', which was written not long before *Men Among the Ruins*, we can see something of the state of Evola's mind immediately after the war. Pessimism was something always alien to Evola's conception of life, but in this essay we can see Evola surveying the political forces at work in 1950 and realising that none of them can possibly hold any interest for those of a traditional nature. With the destruction of the hierarchical and heroic vision of Fascism, nothing was left to choose from on the political stage but the two competing ideologies of egalitarianism: democratic capitalism and Communism, both of which sought to dehumanise the individual. Moreover, Evola observes that war in the technological age has been reduced to the combat between machinery, and, as such, the opportunities for heroic transcendence offered by war in earlier times are no longer available. Therefore, the struggle for an individual seeking to experience heroism will not be one of politics, or even of combat on the battlefield, but rather, it will consist of the heroic individual in conflict with the phenomenon of 'total war' itself, in which the idea of humanity faces possible annihilation. This is, indeed, the predicament in which we have all found ourselves since 1945, the year when humanity not only harnessed the ability to extinguish itself, but also began to face the prospect of becoming lost within ever-multiplying machinery of our own creation. With no significant political forces opposing the conversion of our world into a universal marketplace, the conflict of our time is the struggle to retain one's humanity in an increasingly artificial world. That is the only battle that retains any genuine significance from a traditional perspective.

Most of the footnotes to the texts were added by myself. A small number of footnotes added by Evola himself were included with some of the essays and have been so indicated.

The Forms of Warlike Heroism[1]

The fundamental principle underlying all justifications of war, from the point of view of human personality, is 'heroism'. War, it is said, offers man the opportunity to awaken the hero who sleeps within him. War breaks the routine of comfortable life; by means of its severe ordeals, it offers a transfiguring knowledge of life, life according to death. The moment the individual succeeds in living as a hero, even if it is the final moment of his earthly life, weighs infinitely more on the scale of values than a protracted existence spent consuming monotonously among the trivialities of cities. From a spiritual point of view, these possibilities make up for the negative and destructive tendencies of war, which are one-sidedly and tendentiously highlighted by pacifist materialism. War makes one realise the relativity of human life and therefore also the law of a 'more-than-life', and thus war has always an anti-materialist value, a spiritual value.

Such considerations have indisputable merit and cut off the chattering of humanitarianism, sentimental grizzling, the protests of the champions of the 'immortal principles', and of the 'International' of the heroes of the pen. Nevertheless, it must be acknowledged that, in order to define fully the conditions under which the spiritual aspect of war actually becomes apparent, it is necessary to examine the matter further, and to outline a sort

---

1 Originally published on 25 May 1935 as 'Sulle forme dell'eroismo guerriero' in 'Diorama mensile', *Il Regime Fascista*.

of 'phenomenology of warrior experience', distinguishing various forms and arranging them hierarchically so as to highlight the aspect which must be regarded as paramount for the heroic experience.

To arrive at this result, it is necessary to recall a doctrine with which the regular readers of 'Diorama' will already be familiar, which – bear in mind – is not the product of some particular, personal, philosophical construction, but rather that of actual data, positive and objective in nature. It is the doctrine of the hierarchical quadripartition, which interprets most recent history as an involutionary fall from each of the four hierarchical degrees to the next. This quadripartition – it must be recalled – is what, in all traditional civilisations, gave rise to four different castes: the slaves, the bourgeois middle-class, the warrior aristocracy, and bearers of a pure, spiritual authority. Here, 'caste' does not mean – as most assume – something artificial and arbitrary, but rather the 'place' where individuals, sharing the same nature, the same type of interest and vocation, the same primordial qualification, gather. A specific 'truth', a specific function, defines the castes, in their normal state, and not vice versa: this is not therefore a matter of privileges and ways of life being monopolised on the basis of a social constitution more or less artificially and unnaturally maintained. The underlying principle behind all the formative institutions in such societies, at least in their more authentic historical forms, is that there does not exist one simple, universal way of living one's life, but several distinct spiritual ways, appropriate respectively to the warrior, the bourgeois and the slave, and that, when the social functions and distributions actually correspond to this articulation, there is – according to the classic expression – an order *secundum equum et bonum*.[2]

This order is 'hierarchical' in that it implies a natural dependence of the inferior ways of life on the superior ones – and, along with dependence, co-operation; the task of the superior is to attain expression and personhood on a purely spiritual basis. Only such cases, in which this straight and normal relationship

---

2   Latin: 'according to truth and justice'. This has long been a common legal maxim.

of subordination and co-operation exists are healthy, as is made clear by the analogy of the human organism, which is unsound if, by some chance, the physical element (slaves) or the element of vegetative life (bourgeoisie) or that of the uncontrolled animal will (warriors) takes the primary and guiding place in the life of a man, and is sound only when spirit constitutes the central and ultimate point of reference for the remaining faculties – which, however, are not denied a partial autonomy, with lives and subordinate rights of their own within the unity of the whole.

Since we are not talking about just any old hierarchy, but about 'true' hierarchy, which means that what is above and rules is really what is superior, it is necessary to refer to systems of civilisation in which, at the centre, there is a spiritual elite, and the ways of life of the slaves, the bourgeois, and the warriors derive their ultimate meaning and supreme justification from reference to the principle which is the specific heritage of this spiritual elite, and manifest this principle in their material activity. However, an abnormal state is arrived at if the centre shifts, so that the fundamental point of reference, instead of being the spiritual principle, is that of the servile caste, the bourgeoisie, or the warriors. Each of these castes manifests its own hierarchy and a certain code of co-operation, but each is more unnatural, more distorted, and more subversive than the last, until the process reaches its limit – that is, a system in which the vision of life characteristic of the slaves comes to orientate everything and to imbue itself with all the surviving elements of social wholeness.

Politically, this involutionary process is quite visible in Western history, and it can be traced through into the most recent times. States of the aristocratic and sacred type have been succeeded by monarchical warrior States, to a large extent already secularised, which in turn have been replaced by states ruled by capitalist oligarchies (bourgeois or merchant caste) and, finally, we have witnessed tendencies towards socialist, collectivist and proletarian states, which have culminated in Russian Bolshevism (the caste of the slaves).

This process is paralleled by transitions from one type of civilisation to another, from one fundamental meaning of life to another. In each phase, every concept, every principle, every institution assumes a different meaning, reflecting the world-view of the predominant caste.

This is also true of 'war', and thus we can approach the task we originally set ourselves, of specifying the varieties of meaning which battle and heroic death can acquire. War has a different face, in accordance with its being placed under the sign of one or another of the castes. While, in the cycle of the first caste, war was justified by spiritual motives, and showed clearly its value as a path to supernatural accomplishment and the attainment of immortality by the hero (this being the motive of the 'holy war'), in the cycle of the warrior aristocracies they fought for the honour and power of some particular prince, to whom they showed a loyalty which was willingly associated with the pleasure of war for war's sake. With the passage of power into the hands of the bourgeoisie, there was a deep transformation; at this point, the concept of the nation materialises and democratises itself, and an anti-aristocratic and naturalistic conception of the homeland is formed, so that the warrior is replaced by the soldier-citizen, who fights simply for the defence or the conquest of land; wars, however, generally remain slyly driven by supremacist motives or tendencies originating within the economic and industrial order. Finally, the last stage, in which leadership passes into the hands of the slaves, has already been able to realise – in Bolshevism – another meaning of war, which finds expression in the following, characteristic words of Lenin: 'The war between nations is a childish game, preoccupied by the survival of a middle class which does not concern us. True war, our war, is the world revolution for the destruction of the bourgeoisie and the triumph of the proletariat.'

Given all this, it is obvious that the term 'hero' is a common denominator which embraces very different types and meanings. The readiness to die, to sacrifice one's own life, may be the sole prerequisite, from the technical and collectivist point of view, but also from the point of view of what today, rather brutally, has come to be referred to as 'cannon fodder'. However, it is also obvious that it is not from this point of view that war can claim any real spiritual value as regards the individual, once the latter does not appear as 'fodder' but as a personality – as is the Roman standpoint. This latter standpoint is only possible provided that there is a double relationship of means to ends – that is to say, when, on the one hand, the individual appears as a means with respect to a war and its material ends, but, simultaneously, when a war, in its turn, is a means for the individual, as an opportunity or path for the end of his spiritual accomplishment, favoured by heroic experience. There is then a synthesis, an energy and, with it, an utmost efficiency.

If we proceed with this train of thought, it becomes rather clear from what has been said above that not all wars have the same possibilities. This is because of analogies, which are not merely abstractions, but which act positively along paths invisible to most people, between the collective character predominating in the various cycles of civilisation and the element which corresponds to this character in the whole of the human entity. If, in the eras of the merchants and slaves, forces prevail which correspond to the energies which define man's pre-personal, physical, instinctive, 'telluric', organic-vital part, then, in the eras of the warriors and spiritual leaders, forces find expression which correspond, respectively, to what in man is character and volitional personality, and what in him is spiritualised personality, personality realised according to its supernatural destiny. Because of all the transcendent factors it arouses in them, it is obvious that, in a war, the majority cannot but collectively undergo an awakening, corresponding more or less to the predominant influence within the order of the causes which have been most decisive for the outbreak of that war. Individually, the heroic experience then leads to different points of arrival: more precisely, to three primary such points.

These points correspond, basically, to three possible types of relation in which the warrior caste and its principle can find themselves with respect to the other manifestations already considered. In the normal state, they are subordinate to the spiritual principle, and then there breaks out a heroism which leads to supra-life, to supra-personhood. The warrior principle may, however, construct its own form, refusing to recognise anything as superior to it, and then the heroic experience takes on a quality which is 'tragic': insolent, steel-tempered, but without light. Personality remains, and strengthens, but, at the same time, so does the limit constituted by its naturalistic and simply human nature. Nevertheless, this type of 'hero' shows a certain greatness, and, naturally, for the types hierarchically inferior to the warrior, i.e., the bourgeois and the slave types, this war and this heroism already mean overcoming, elevation, accomplishment. The third case involves a degraded warrior principle, which has passed into the service of hierarchically inferior elements (the castes beneath it). In such cases, heroic experience is united, almost fatally, to an evocation, and an eruption, of instinctual, sub-personal, collective, irrational forces, so that there occurs, basically, a lesion and a regression of the personality of the individual, who can only live life in a passive manner, driven either by necessity or by the suggestive power of myths and passionate impulses. For example, the notorious stories of Remarque[3] reflect only possibilities of this latter kind; they recount the stories of human types who, driven to war by fake idealisms, at last realise that reality is something very different – they do not become base, nor deserters, but all that impels them forward throughout the most terrible tests are elemental forces, impulses, instincts, and reactions, in which there is not much human remaining, and which do not know any moment of light.

In a preparation for war which must be not only material, but also spiritual, it is necessary to recognise all of this with a clear and unflinching gaze in order to be able to orientate souls and

---

3   Erich Maria Remarque (1898-1970) was a German writer who served in the First World War. His most well-known work is his 1927 novel, *All Quiet on the Western Front*, which depicted the war in horrific and pacifist terms.

energies towards the higher solution, the only one which corresponds to the ideals from which Fascism draws its inspiration.

Fascism appears to us as a reconstructive revolution, in that it affirms an aristocratic and spiritual concept of the nation, as against both socialist and internationalist collectivism, and the democratic and demagogic notion of the nation. In addition, its scorn for the economic myth and its elevation of the nation in practice to the degree of 'warrior nation', marks positively the first degree of this reconstruction, which is to re-subordinate the values of the ancient castes of the 'merchants' and 'slaves' to the values of the immediately higher caste. The next step would be the spiritualisation of the warrior principle itself. The point of departure would then be present to develop a heroic experience in the sense of the highest of the three possibilities mentioned above. To understand how such a higher, spiritual possibility, which has been properly experienced in the greatest civilisations that have preceded us, and which, to speak the truth, is what makes apparent to us their constant and universal aspect, is more than just studious erudition. This is what we will deal with in our following writings, in which we shall focus essentially on the traditions peculiar to ancient and Medieval Romanity.

The Sacrality of War[1]

In our previous article, we have seen that the phenomenon of warrior heroism has different forms, and can have fundamentally different meanings, as seen from the point of view of a conception intended to establish the values of true spirituality.

Resuming our argument from that point, we shall begin by indicating some conceptions related to our ancient traditions, the Roman traditions. One generally has only a secular idea of the values of ancient Rome. According to this idea, the Roman was merely a soldier, in the most limited sense of the word, and it was by means of his merely soldierly qualities, together with a fortunate combination of circumstances, that he conquered the world. This is a false opinion.

In the first place, right up until the end, the Romans considered it an article of faith that divine forces both created and protected the greatness of Rome – the *imperium*[2] and the Aeternitas.[3] Those who want to limit themselves to a 'positive' point of view are obliged to replace this perception, deeply felt by the Romans, with a mystery; the mystery, that is, that a handful of men, without any really compelling reasons, without even ideas of 'land' or

---

1 Originally published on 8 June 1935 as 'Sacrità della guerra' in 'Diorama mensile', *Il Regime Fascista*.

2 *Imperium*, which was the power vested in the leaders of Rome, was believed to originate from divine sanction.

3 Aeternitas Imperii, meaning 'the eternity of Roman rule', was a goddess who looked after the preservation of the Empire.

'homeland', and without any of the myths or passions to which the moderns so willingly resort to justify war and promote heroism, kept moving, further and further, from one country to the next, following a strange and irresistible impulse, basing everything on an 'ascesis of power'. According to the unanimous testimony of all the Classical authors, the early Romans were highly religious – *nostri maiores religiossimi mortales*, Sallust recalls[4] – and Cicero[5] and Gellius[6] repeat his view – but this religiosity of theirs was not confined to an abstract and isolated sphere, but pervaded their experience in its entirety, including in itself the world of action, and therefore also the world of the warrior experience.

A special sacred college in Rome, the Feciales, presided over a quite definite system of rites which provided the mystical counterpart to every war, from its declaration to its termination. More generally, it is certain that one of the principles of the military art of the Romans required them not to allow themselves to be compelled to engage in battle before certain mystical signs had defined, so to speak, its 'moment'. Because of the mental distortions and prejudices resulting from modern education, most people of today would naturally be inclined to see in this an extrinsic, superstitious superstructure. The most benevolent may see in it an eccentric fatalism, but it is neither of these. The essence of the augural art practiced by the Roman patriciate, like similar disciplines, with more or less the same characters which can easily be found in the cycle of the greater Indo-European civilisations, was not the discovery of 'fates' to be followed with superstitious passivity: rather, it was the knowledge of points of juncture with invisible influences, the use of which the forces of

---

4   'Our ancestors were a most devout race of men', from Sallust's *The Conspiracy of Catiline,* chapter 12. In this passage Sallust praises the devotional character of the early Romans in opposition to the Romans of his day, whom he called 'the basest of mankind'. Sallust (86-34 BC) was a noted Roman historian.

5   Marcus Tullius Cicero (106-43 BCE) was a philosopher and famed orator in the Roman Republic.

6   Aulus Gellius (c. 125-c. 180 AD) was a Roman author whose only surviving work is his *Attic Nights*, which is a commonplace book of notes taken from various other sources that he had read or heard about.

men could be developed, multiplied, and led to act on a higher plane, in addition to the everyday one, thus – when the harmony was perfect – bringing about the removal of every obstacle and every resistance within an event-complex which was material and spiritual at the same time. In the light of this knowledge, it cannot be doubted that Roman values, the Roman 'ascesis of power', necessarily possessed a spiritual and sacred aspect, and that they were regarded not only as a means to military and temporal greatness, but also as a means of contact and connection with supernal forces.

If it were appropriate to do so here, we could produce various materials in support of this thesis. We will limit ourselves, however, to mentioning that the ceremony of the triumph in Rome had a character which was far more religious than militaristic in a secular sense, and that many elements seem to show that the Roman attributed the victory of his leaders less to their simply human attributes than to a transcendent force manifesting itself in a real and efficient manner through them, their heroism and sometimes their sacrifice (as in the rite known as the *devotio*, in which the leaders sacrificed themselves).[7] The victor, in the aforesaid ceremony of the triumph, put on the insignia of the supreme God of the Capitol[8] as if he was a divine image, and went in procession to place the triumphal laurels of his victory in the hands of this God, as if to say that the latter was the true victor.

Finally, one of the origins of the imperial apotheosis, that is to say, of the feeling that an immortal *numen*[9] was concealed in the Emperor, is undoubtedly the experience of the warrior: the

---

7   In the *devotio*, a Roman general would offer to sacrifice his own life in a battle in order to ensure victory.

8   The Capitolium was a temple on one of the seven hills of Rome which was dedicated to a triad of deities. The original triad consisted of Jupiter, Mars and Quinrus. Later it was comprised of Jupiter, Juno and Minerva.

9   'The *numen*, unlike the notion of *deus* (as it later came to be understood), is not a being or a person, but a sheer power that is capable of producing effects, of acting, and of manifesting itself. The sense of the real presence of such powers, or *numina*, as something simultaneously transcendent and yet immanent, marvelous yet fearful, constituted the substance of the original experience of the "sacred"'. From Julius Evola, *Revolt Against the Modern World* (Rochester: Inner Traditions, 1995), p. 42.

imperator was originally the military leader,[10] acclaimed on the battlefield in the moment of victory: in this moment, he seemed transfigured by a force from above, fearful and wonderful, which imposed precisely the feeling of the *numen*. This view, we may add, is not peculiar to Rome, but is found throughout the whole of Classical Mediterranean antiquity, and it was not restricted to victors in war, but sometimes applied also to the winners of the Olympic Games and of the bloody fights of the circus. In the Hellades,[11] the myth of heroes merges with mystical doctrines, such as Orphism,[12] which significantly unite the character of the victorious warrior and the initiate, victor over death, in the same symbolism.

These are precise indications of a heroism and a system of values which develop into various more or less self-consciously spiritual paths, paths sanctified not only by the glorious material conquest which they mediate, but also by the fact that they represent a sort of ritual evocation involving conquest of the intangible.

Let us consider some other evidence of this tradition, which, by its very nature, is metaphysical: elements such as 'race' cannot therefore possess more than a secondary, contingent place in it. We say this because, in our next article, we intend to deal with the 'holy war' practiced by the warriors of the 'Holy Roman Empire'.[13] That civilisation, as is well known, represents a point of creative convergence between various components: Roman, Christian, and Nordic.

---

10 This was the case in the Roman Republic. During the Roman Empire, the title of imperator was only granted to the Emperor, and occasionally members of his family.

11 The plural form of Hellas, which is the ancient name of Greece.

12 Orphism was a religion in ancient Greece which differed in a number of respects from the popular religion, said to have been founded by the poet Orpheus who descended to Hades and then returned.

13 The Holy Roman Empire, as it came to be known, was founded in 962 AD and survived in various forms until 1806. Its territorial makeup was always in flux, but at its peak it consisted of Central Europe, including modern-day Germany, as well as parts of present-day Italy and France. In spite of its name, Rome was rarely ever part of the Empire, and there was no direct connection between it and the original Roman Empire.

We have already discussed the relevant features of the first of these components (i.e., the Roman). The Christian component will appear with the features of a knightly, supranational heroism as the Crusade. The Nordic component remains to be indicated. To avoid alarming our readers unnecessarily we have stated at the outset that what we refer to has, essentially, a supra-racial character, and is not therefore calculated to encourage the stance of any self-styled 'special' people towards others. To limit ourselves to one hint at what sort of thing we here mean to exclude, we will say that, surprising as it may seem, in the more or less frantic Nordic revivalism celebrated today *ad usum delphini*[14] by National Socialist Germany, we find mainly a deformation and vulgarisation of Nordic traditions as they existed originally, and as they could still be found in those princes who considered it a great honour to be able to say of themselves that they were Romans, although of the Teutonic race. Instead, for many racist writers today, 'Nordic' has come to mean anti-Roman, and 'Roman' has come to mean, more or less, 'Jewish'.

Having said that, we think it is appropriate to reproduce this significant formula of exhortation to the warrior as found in the ancient Celtic tradition: 'Fight for your land, and accept death if need be, since death is a victory and a liberation to the soul.'

The expression *mors triumphalis*[15] in our own Classical tradition corresponds to this concept. As for the properly Nordic tradition, well-known to all is the part which concerns Valhalla, the seat of celestial immortality, reserved for the 'free' divine stock and the heroes fallen on the battlefield ('Valhalla' means literally 'from the palace of the chosen'). The Lord of this symbolic seat, Odin or Wotan, appears in the *Ynglingasaga* as the one who, by his symbolic self-sacrifice on the 'world tree', showed the heroes how to reach the divine sojourn, where they live eternally as on a bright peak, which remains in perpetual sunlight, above every cloud.

---

14 'For the use of the Dauphin', after a practice of censoring the Greek and Roman classics which was promoted by Louis XIV for the education of his son, which called for the removal of supposedly offensive passages from them.

15 Latin: 'triumphal death'.

According to this tradition, no sacrifice or form of worship was more appreciated by the supreme God, and rich in supra-mundane fruits, than that which is performed by the warrior who fights and falls on the battlefield. But this is not all. The spirits of the fallen heroes would add their forces to the phalanx of those who assist the 'celestial heroes' in fighting in the *ragnarökk*, that is to say, the fate of the 'darkening of the divine', which, according to these teachings, and also according to the Hellenes (Hesiod),[16] has threatened the world since time immemorial.

We will see this motif reappear, in a different form, in the Medieval legends which relate to the 'last battle', which the immortal emperor will fight. Here, to illustrate the universality of these elements, we will point out the similarity between these ancient Nordic conceptions (which, let us say in passing, Wagner[17] has rendered unrecognisable by means of his hazy, bombastic, characteristically Teutonic romanticism) and the ancient Iranian, and later Persian, conceptions. Many may be astonished to hear that the well-known Valkyries, which choose the souls of the warriors destined for Valhalla, are only the transcendental personification of parts of the warriors themselves, parts which find their exact equivalent in the Fravashi, of which the Iranian-Persian traditions speak – the Fravashi, also represented as women of light and stormy virgins of battle, which personify more or less the supernatural forces by means of which the human natures of the warriors 'faithful to the God of Light' can transfigure themselves and bring about terrible, overwhelming and bloody victories. The Iranian tradition also includes the symbolic conception of a divine figure –Mithra, described as 'the warrior who never sleeps' – who, at the head of his faithful Fravashi, fights against the emissaries

---

16 Hesiod (approx. 7th century BC) was an early Greek poet. His most famous work, the *Works and Days*, outlines the cyclical Five Ages of Man, beginning with the utopian Golden Age and ending in the apocalyptic Iron Age.

17 Richard Wagner (1813-1883), the German composer, whose works were very influential in all spheres of European culture at this time. Evola no doubt has in mind Wagner's tetralogy of music dramas, *The Ring of the Nibelungen*, the *libretto* of which is based on the ancient Norse myths.

of the dark god until the coming of the Saoshyant, Lord of the future kingdom of 'triumphant' peace.

These elements of ancient Indo-European tradition, in which the motifs recur of the sacrality of war and of the hero who does not really die but becomes part of a mystical army in a cosmic battle, have had a perceptible effect on certain elements of Christianity – at least that Christianity which could realistically adopt the motto: *vita est militia super terram*,[18] and recognise not only salvation through humility, charity, hope and the rest, but also that – by including the heroic element, in our case – 'the Kingdom of Heaven can be taken by storm'. It is precisely this convergence of motifs which gave birth to the spiritual conception of 'Greater War' peculiar to the medieval age, which we shall discuss in our next article in 'Diorama', where we shall deal more closely with the interior, individual, but nevertheless topical aspect of these teachings.

---

18 Latin: 'life is a struggle on Earth'.

The Meaning of the Crusades[1]

L et us resume our examination of those traditions concerning
heroism in which war is regarded as a path of spiritual
realisation in the strictest sense of the term, and thus acquires a
transcendent justification and purpose. We have already discussed
the conceptions of the ancient Roman world in this respect. We
then described the Nordic traditions regarding the immortalising
character of the truly heroic death on the battlefield. It was
necessary to examine these traditions before considering the
medieval world, since, as is generally recognised, the Middle Ages,
as a culture, arose from the synthesis of three elements; firstly,
Roman; secondly, Nordic; and thirdly, Christian.

Thus, we are now in a position to examine the idea of the
'sacredness of War' as the Western Medieval age knew and cul-
tivated it. As should be evident, we here refer to the Crusades
as understood in their deepest sense, not the sense claimed by
historical materialists, according to which they are mere effects
of economical and ethnic determinisms, nor the sense claimed by
'developed' minds, according to which they are mere phenomena
of superstition and religious exaltation – nor, finally, will we even
regard them as simply Christian phenomena. In respect to this last
point it is necessary not to lose sight of the correct relationship
between means and ends. It is often said that, in the Crusades, the

1   Originally published on 9 July 1935 as 'Significato della Crociata' in 'Diorama
mensile', *Il Regime Fascista*.

Christian faith made use of the heroic spirit of Western chivalry. However, the opposite is the truth: that is to say, the Christian faith, and the relative and contingent imperatives of the religious struggle against the 'infidel' and the 'liberation' of the 'Temple' and 'Holy Land', were merely the means which allowed the heroic spirit to manifest itself, to affirm itself, and to realise a sort of ascesis, distinct from that of the contemplative, but no less rich in spiritual fruits. Most of the knights who gave their energies and their blood for the 'holy war' had only the vaguest ideas and the sketchiest theological knowledge regarding the doctrine for which they fought.

However, the cultural context of the Crusades contained a wealth of elements able to confer upon them a higher, spiritually symbolic meaning. Transcendent myths resurfaced from the subconscious in the soul of Western chivalry: the conquest of the 'Holy Land' located 'beyond the sea' was much more closely associated than many people have imagined with the ancient saga according to which 'in the distant East, where the Sun rises, lies the sacred city where death does not exist, and the fortunate heroes who are able to reach it enjoy celestial serenity and perpetual life'.

Moreover, the struggle against Islam had, by its nature and from its inception, the significance of an ascetic test. 'This was not merely a struggle for the kingdoms of the earth', wrote the famous historian of the Crusades, Kugler,[2] 'but a struggle for the Kingdom of Heaven: the Crusades were not a thing of men, but rather of God – therefore, they should not be thought of in the same way as other human events.'

Sacred war, according to an old chronicler, should be compared to 'a bath like that in the fire of purgatory, but before death'. Those who died in the Crusades were compared symbolically by Popes and priests to 'gold tested three times and refined seven times in the fire', a purifying ordeal so powerful that it opened the way to the supreme Lord.

---

2   Bernhard Kugler, *Geschichte der Kreuzzüge* (Berlin: G. Grote, 1880). No English
    translation exists.

'Never forget this oracle', wrote Saint Bernard,[3] 'whether we live, or whether we die, we belong to the Lord. It is a glory for you never to leave the battle [unless] covered with laurels. But it is an even greater glory to earn on the battlefield an immortal crown [...] Oh fortunate condition, in which death can be approached without fear, waited for with impatience, and received with a serene heart.' It was promised that the Crusader would attain an absolute glory – *glorie asolue,* in the Provençal tongue – and that he would find 'rest in paradise' – *conquerre lit en paradis* – that is to say, he would achieve the supra-life, the supernatural state of existence, something beyond religious representation. In this respect, Jerusalem, the coveted goal of the conquest, appeared in a double aspect, as an earthly city and as a symbolic, celestial and intangible city – and the Crusade gained an inner value independent of all outer integuments, supports and apparent motives.

Besides, the greatest contribution in manpower was supplied to the Crusades by knightly orders such as the Templars and the Knights of Saint John, which were made up of men who, like the monk or the Christian ascetic, had learned to despise the vanity of this life; warriors weary of the world, who had seen everything and enjoyed everything, withdrew into such orders, thus making themselves ready for an absolute action, free from the interests of common, temporal life, and also of political life in the narrow sense. Urban VIII[4] addressed chivalry as the supra-national community of those who were 'ready to run to war wherever it might break out, and to bring to it the fear of their arms in defence of honour and of justice'. They should answer the call to 'sacred war' all the more readily, according to one of the writers of the time, since its reward is not an earthly fief, always revocable and contingent, but a 'celestial fief'.

---

3   Saint Bernard of Clairvaux (1090-1153), a French abbot who was extremely influential in raising the Second Crusade. He also helped to formulate the Rule of the Knights Templar.

4   Urban VIII (1568-1644) was Pope from 1623 until his death, during the Thirty Years' War. He was the last Pope to use armed force in an effort to increase the area under Papal authority. He was also the Pope who condemned Galileo for his theory of heliocentrism.

Moreover, the course of the Crusades, with all its broader implications for the general ideology of the time, led to a purification and internalisation of the spirit of the enterprise. Given the initial conviction that the war for the 'true faith' could not but have a victorious result, the first military setbacks undergone by the Crusader armies were a source of surprise and dismay; but, in the end, they served to bring to light the higher aspect of 'sacred war'. The unhappy fate of a Crusade was compared by the clerics of Rome to the misfortunes of virtue, which are made good only in *another life*. But, by taking this approach, they were already close to recognising something superior to both victory and defeat, and to according the highest importance to the distinctive aspect of heroic action which is accomplished independently of any visible and material fruits, almost in the sense of an offering, which draws, from the virile sacrifice of all human elements, the immortalising 'absolute glory'.

One sees that in this way they approached a plane that was supra-traditional, in the most strict, historical and religious sense of the word 'tradition'. The particular religious faith, the immediate purposes, the antagonistic spirit, were revealed clearly as mere means, as inessential in themselves, as the precise nature of a fuel which is used for the sole purpose of reviving and feeding a flame. What remained at the centre, however, was the sacred value of war. Thus it became possible to recognise that the opponents of the moment accorded to battle the same traditional meaning.

In this way and despite everything, the Crusades were able to enrich the cultural exchange between the Ghibelline[5] West and the Arabic East (itself the centre of more ancient traditional elements), an exchange whose significance is much greater than most historians have yet recognised. As the knights of the crusading orders found themselves in the presence of knights of Arab orders

---

5   The Ghibellines were a faction in the Holy Roman Empire who favoured the imperial power of the Hohenstaufen throne over the power of the Vatican, as was supported by their rivals, the Guelphs. Evola saw this conflict as highlighting the distinction between priestly and royal authority in the state, since he believed the Ghibelline view to be the only valid one from a traditional perspective. He discusses this at length in *Revolt Against the Modern World*.

which were almost their doubles, manifesting correspondences in ethics, customs, and sometimes even symbols, so the 'sacred war' which had impelled the two civilisations against each other in the name of their respective religions, led them at the same time to meet, that is to say, to realise that, despite having as starting points two different faiths, they had eventually accorded to war the identical, independent value of spirituality.

In our next article, we shall study the way in which, from the premises of his faith, the ancient Arab Knight ascended to the same supra-traditional point which the Crusader Knight attained by his heroic asceticism.

For now, however, we would like to deal with a different point. Those who regard the Crusades, with indignation, as among the most extravagant episodes of the 'dark' Middle Ages, have not even the slightest suspicion that what they call 'religious fanaticism' was the visible sign of the presence and effectiveness of a sensitivity and decisiveness, the absence of which is more characteristic of true barbarism. *In fact, the man of the Crusades was able to rise, to fight and to die for a purpose which, in its essence, was supra-political and supra-human,* and to serve on a front defined no longer by what is particularistic, but rather by what is universal. This remains a value, an unshakeable point of reference.

Naturally, this must not be misunderstood to mean that the transcendent motive may be used as an excuse for the warrior to become indifferent, to forget the duties inherent in his belonging to a race and to a fatherland. This is not at all our point, which concerns rather the essentially deeply disparate meanings according to which actions and sacrifices can be experienced, despite the fact that, from the external point of view, they may be absolutely the same. There is a radical difference between the one who engages in warfare simply as such, and the one who simultaneously engages in 'sacred war' and finds in it a higher experience, both desired and desirable for the spirit.

We must add that, although this difference is primarily an interior one, nevertheless, because the powers of interiority are able to find expression also in exteriority, effects derive from it also on the exterior plane, specifically in the following respects:

First of all, in an 'indomitability' of the heroic impulse: the one who experiences heroism spiritually is pervaded with a metaphysical tension, an impetus, whose object is 'infinite', and which, therefore, will carry him perpetually forward, beyond the capacity of one who fights from necessity, fights as a trade, or is spurred by natural instincts or external suggestion.

Secondly, the one who fights according to the sense of 'sacred war' is spontaneously beyond every particularism and exists in a spiritual climate which, at any given moment, may very well give rise and life to a supra-national unity of action. This is precisely what occurred in the Crusades when princes and dukes of every land gathered in the heroic and sacred enterprise, regardless of their particular utilitarian interests or political divisions, bringing about for the first time a great European unity, true to the common civilisation and to the very principle of the Holy Roman Empire.

Now, in this respect as well, if we are able to leave aside the 'integument', if we are able to isolate the essential from the contingent, we will find an element whose precious value is not restricted to any particular historical period. To succeed in referring heroic action also to an 'ascetic' plane, and in justifying the former according to the latter, is to clear the road towards a possible new unity of civilisation, to remove every antagonism conditioned by matter, to prepare the environment for great distances and for great fronts, and, therefore, to adapt the outer purposes of action gradually to its new spiritual meaning, when it is no longer a land and the temporal ambitions of a land for which one fights, but a superior principle of civilisation, a foreshadowing of what, even though itself metaphysical, moves ever forward, beyond every limit, beyond every danger, beyond every destruction.

The Greater War and the Lesser War[1]

Our readers should not consider it strange that, after having examined a group of Western traditions relating to holy war – that is to say, to war as a spiritual value – we now propose to examine this same concept as expressed in the Islamic tradition. In fact, for our purposes (as we have often pointed out) it is interesting to clarify the objective value of a principle by means of the demonstration of its universality, that is to say, of its conformity to the principle of *quod ubique, quod ab omnibus, et quod semper.*[2] Only in this way can we establish with certainty that some values are absolutely independent of the views of any particular thinker, and also that, in their essence, they are superior to the particular forms which they have assumed in order to manifest themselves in one or another historical tradition. The more we manage to demonstrate the inner correspondence of such forms and their unique principle, the more deeply the reader will become able to delve into his own tradition, to possess it fully, and to understand it from its own unique metaphysical point of origin.

Historically, in order to comprehend what concerns us here, it must first be understood that the Islamic tradition, rather than having such a unique metaphysical point of origin, is essentially

---

1   Originally published on 21 July 1935 as 'La grande e la piccola guerra' in 'Diorama mensile', *Il Regime Fascista*.

2   Latin: 'that which is accepted everywhere, by everyone, and always'. This is an axiom of the Catholic Church.

41

dependent upon its inheritance of the Persian tradition – Persia, as is well known, having possessed one of the highest pre-European civilisations. The original Mazdaist conception of religion, as military service under the sign of the 'God of Light', and of existence as a continuous, relentless struggle to rescue beings and things from the control of an anti-god, is at the centre of the Persian vision of life, and should be considered as the metaphysical counterpart and spiritual background to the warrior enterprises which culminated in the creation of the empire of the 'kings of kings' by the Persians. After the fall of Persia's power, echoes of such traditions persisted in the cycle of Medieval Arabian civilisation in forms which became slightly more materialistic and sometimes exaggerated, yet not to such an extent that their original elements of spirituality were entirely lost.

We bring up traditions of that kind here, above all because they introduce a concept which is very useful in further clarifying the order of ideas set out in our latest articles; namely, the concept of the 'greater' or 'holy war', as distinct from the 'lesser war', but at the same time as related to the latter in a special manner. The distinction itself derives from a saying of the Prophet, who, returning from a battle, declared, 'I return now from the lesser to the greater war.'[3]

The lesser war here corresponds to the exoteric war, the bloody battle which is fought with material arms against the enemy, against the 'barbarian', against an inferior race over whom a superior right is claimed, or, finally, when the event is motivated by a religious justification, against the 'infidel'. No matter how terrible and tragic the events, no matter how huge the destruction, this war, metaphysically, *still remains a 'lesser war'*. The 'greater' or 'holy war' is, contrarily, of the interior and intangible order – it is the war which is fought against the enemy, the 'barbarian', the 'infidel', whom everyone bears in himself, or whom everyone can see arising in himself on every occasion that he tries to subject

3   This is recorded in the *Hadith* (oral traditions) of the Prophet Muhammad – specifically, in the *Tarikh Baghdad* of Khatib al-Baghdadi (13:493, 523). The text goes on to say that Muhammad's followers asked him, 'What is the greater war?', to which he replied, 'The war against the lower part of our nature.'

his whole being to a spiritual law. Appearing in the forms of craving, partiality, passion, instinctuality, weakness and inward cowardice, the enemy within the natural man must be vanquished, its resistance broken, chained and subjected to the spiritual man, this being the condition of reaching inner liberation, the 'triumphant peace' which allows one to participate in what is beyond both life and death.

Some may say that this is simply asceticism. The greater, holy war is the ascesis which has always been a philosophical goal. It could be tempting to add as well: it is the path of those who wish to escape from the world and who, using the excuse of inner liberation, become a herd of pacifist cowards. This is not at all the way things are. After the distinction between the two types of war there is their synthesis. It is a feature of heroic traditions that they prescribe the 'lesser war', that is to say the real, bloody war, as an instrument in the realisation of the 'greater' or 'holy war'; so much so that, finally, both become one and the same thing.

Thus, in Islam, 'holy war' – *jihad* – and 'the path of God' are interchangeable terms. The one who fights is on the 'path of God'. A well-known and quite characteristic saying of this tradition is, 'The blood of heroes is closer to the Lord than the ink of scholars and the prayers of the pious.'[4]

Once again, as in the traditions already reviewed by us, as in the Roman ascesis of power and in the classical *mors triumphalis*, action attains the value of an inner overcoming and of an approximation to a life no longer mixed with darkness, contingency, uncertainty and death. In more concrete terms, the predicaments, risks and ordeals peculiar to the events of war bring about an emergence of the inner 'enemy', which, in the forms of the instinct of self-preservation, cowardice, cruelty, pity and blind riotousness, arise as obstacles to be vanquished just as one fights the outer enemy. It is clear from this that the decisive point is constituted by one's inner orientation, one's unshakeable persistence in what is spiritual

---

4 I am uncertain of the origin of this saying, but it is contradicted by another Hadith taken from the *Al-Jaami' al-Saghir* of Imam al-Suyuti: 'The ink of the scholar is holier than the blood of the martyr.'

in this double struggle, so that an irresistible and blind changing
of oneself into a sort of wild animal does not occur, but, instead,
a way is found of not letting the deepest forces escape, a way
of seeing to it that one is never overwhelmed inwardly, that one
always remains supreme master of oneself, and, precisely because
of this sovereignty, one remains able to affirm himself against
every possible limitation. In a tradition to which we will dedicate
our next article, this situation is represented by a most characteristic symbol: the warrior is accompanied by an impassive divine
being who, without fighting, leads and guides him in his struggle,
side by side with him in the same war chariot. This symbol is the
personified expression of a duality of principles, which the true
hero, from whom something sacred always emanates, maintains
unceasingly within himself.

To return to the Islamic tradition, we can read in its principal
text, 'So let those who sell the life of this world for the Next
World fight in the Way of Allah. If someone fights in the Way
of Allah, whether he is killed or is victorious, We will pay him an
immense reward'[5] (4:74).

The metaphysical premises for this are prescribed as follows:
'Fight in the Way of Allah against those who fight you' (2:190);
'Kill them wherever you come across them' (II, 191); 'Do not
become faint-hearted and call for peace' (47:35); 'The life of this
world is merely a game and a diversion' (47:36); 'But whoever is
tight-fisted is only tight-fisted to himself' (47:38).

This last principle is obviously a parallel to the evangelical text:
'Whoever seeks to save his life will lose it, and whoever loses his
life will preserve it',[6] as is confirmed by these further passages:
'You who have *iman*![7] what is the matter with you that when you
are told, "Go out and fight in the way of Allah", you sink down
heavily to the earth? Are you happier with this world than the

---

5   *The Noble Qur'an: A New Rendering of Its Meaning in English* (Norwich: Bookwork,
    2005), interpreted by Aisha Bewley. All quotes from the *Qur'an* are taken from this
    edition.

6   *Luke* 17:33, as rendered in *Holy Bible: The New King James* (Nashville: T. Nelson,
    1982).

7   Arabic: 'belief'.

Next World?" (9:38); "Say [to the Companions]: "What do you await for us except for one of the two best things [martyrdom or victory]?" (9:52).

These excerpts too are worth noting: 'Fighting is prescribed for you even if it is hateful to you. It may be that you hate something when it is good for you and it may be that you love something when it is bad for you. Allah knows and you do not know' (2:216), and also, "When a *sura*[8] is sent down saying: "Have *iman* in Allah and do *jihad* together with His Messenger", those among them with wealth will ask you to excuse them, saying, "Let us remain with those who stay behind." They are pleased to be with those who stay behind. Their hearts have been stamped so they do not understand. But the Messenger and those who have *iman* along with him have done *jihad* with their wealth and with themselves. They are the people who will have the good things. They are the ones who are successful' (9:86-89).

Therefore we have here a sort of *amor fati*,[9] a mysterious way of intuiting, evoking and heroically resolving one's own destiny in the intimate certainty that, when the 'right intention' is present, when all indolence and cowardice are vanquished, and the leap beyond the lives of oneself and others, beyond happiness and misfortune, is driven by a sense of spiritual destiny and a thirst for the absolute existence, then one has given birth to a force which will not be able to miss the supreme goal. Then the crisis of tragic and heroic death becomes an insignificant contingency which can be expressed, in religious terms, in the following words: 'As for those who fight in the Way of Allah, He will not let their actions go astray. He will guide them and better their condition and He will admit them into the Garden which He has made known to them' (47:4-6).

As if by a circular path the reader is thus brought back to the same ideas which were examined in our previous writings on the subject of tradition, whether classical or Nordic-Medieval: that is to say, to the idea of a privileged immortality reserved for heroes,

---

8   A *sura* is a chapter of the *Qur'an*.

9   Latin: 'love of fate'.

who alone, according to Hesiod, pass on to inhabit symbolic islands, which image forth the bright and intangible existence of the Olympians.[10]

Additionally, in the Islamic tradition, there are frequent references to the idea that some warriors fallen in the 'sacred war' are in reality *not dead*,[11] in a sense which is not symbolic in any way, and which need not be referred to supernatural states cut off from the energies and destinies of the living. It is not possible to enter into this domain, which is rather mysterious and requires the support of references which would ill befit the present article. What we can say definitely is that, even today, and particularly in Italy, the rites by which a warrior community declares its most heroically fallen companions still 'present' have regained a special evocative force. He who begins from the belief that everything which, by a process of involution, retains today only an allegorical and, at best, moral character, whereas it originally possessed the value of *reality*, and every rite contained real *action* and not mere 'ceremony' – for him these warrior rites of today could perhaps provide material for meditation, and he could perhaps approach the mystery contained in the teaching already quoted: that is, the idea of heroes who really never died, and the idea of victors who, like the Roman Caesar, remain as 'perpetual victors' at the centre of a human stock.

---

10 The gods of the Greek pantheon.

11 For example, *Qur'an* 1:154: 'Do not say that those who are killed in the Way of Allah are dead. On the contrary, they are alive but you are not aware of it.'

The Metaphysics of War[1]

We will conclude our series of essays for the 'Diorama' on the subject of war as a spiritual value by discussing another tradition within the Indo-European heroic cycle, that of the *Bhagavad-Gita*, which is a very well-known text of ancient Hindu wisdom compiled essentially for the warrior caste.

We have not chosen this text arbitrarily and we would not wish anyone to imagine that we offer a newspaper like the *Regime* articles on exotic subjects as objects of curiosity. Now that our discussion of the Islamic tradition has allowed us to express, in general terms, the idea that the internal or 'greater war' is the attainable counterpart and soul of the external war, so a discussion of the tradition contained in the aforementioned text will allow us to present a clear and concise metaphysical vision of the matter.

On a more exterior plane, such a discussion of the Hindu East (which is the great, heroic East, not that of Theosophists, humanitarian pantheists or old gentlemen in rapture before the various Gandhis and Rabindranath Tagores[2]) will assist also in the

---

1   Originally published on 13 August 1935 as 'Metafisica della guerra' in 'Diorama mensile', *Il Regime Fascista*.

2   Rabindranath Tagore (1861-1941) was a highly influential Bengali artist and philosopher who won the 1913 Nobel Prize in Literature, which brought him great international fame at the time Evola was writing. Although Tagore drew upon his native Hindu tradition in his works, he emphasized the individual over tradition, and integrated elements of artistic modernism into his works. From the perspective of Evola's conception of tradition, therefore, he was a poor representative of the Hindu tradition.

correction of a viewpoint and the supra-traditional understanding which are among the first necessities for the New Italian. For too long we have permitted an artificial antithesis between East and West: artificial because, as Mussolini has already pointed out, it opposes to the East the modern and materialistic West, which, in fact, has little in common with the older, truer and greater Western civilisation. The modern West is just as opposed to the ancient West as it is to the East. As soon as we refer to previous times we are effectively in the presence of an ethnic and cultural heritage which is, to a large extent, common to both, and which can only be described as 'Indo-European'. The original ways of life, the spirituality and the institutions of the first colonisers of India and Iran have many points of contact not only with those of the Hellenic and Nordic peoples, but also with those of the original Romans themselves.

The traditions to which we have previously referred offer examples of this: most notably, a common spiritual conception of how to wage war, how to act and die heroically – contrary to the views of those who, on the basis of prejudices and platitudes, cannot hear of Hindu civilisation without thinking of nirvana, fakirs, escapism, negation of the 'Western' values of personhood and so on.

The text to which we have alluded and on which we will base our discussion is presented in the form of a conversation between the warrior Arjuna and the divine Krishna, who acts as the spiritual master of the former. The conversation takes place shortly before a battle in which Arjuna, the victim of humanitarian scruples, is reluctant to participate. In the previous article we have already indicated that, from a spiritual point of view, the two persons, Arjuna and Krishna, are in reality one. They represent two different parts of the human being – Arjuna the principle of action, and Krishna that of transcendent knowledge. The conversation can thus be understood as a sort of monologue, developing a progressive inner clarification and solution, both in the heroic and the spiritual sense, of the problem of the warrior's activity which poses itself to Arjuna as he prepares for battle.

Now, the pity which prevents the warrior from fighting when he recognises among the ranks of the enemy some of his erstwhile friends and closest relatives is described by Krishna, that is to say by the spiritual principle, as 'impurities...not at all befitting a man who knows the value of life. They lead not to higher planets but to infamy' (2:2).[3]

We have already seen this theme appear many times in the traditional teachings of the West: '[E]ither you will be killed on the battlefield and attain the heavenly planets, or you will conquer and enjoy the earthly kingdom. Therefore, get up with determination and fight' (2:37).

However, along with this, the motif of the 'inner war', to be fought at the same moment, is outlined: 'Thus knowing oneself to be transcendental to the material senses, mind and intelligence, O mighty-armed Arjuna, one should steady the mind by deliberate spiritual intelligence and thus – by spiritual strength – conquer this insatiable enemy known as lust' (3:43).

The internal enemy, which is passion, the animal thirst for life, is thus the counterpart of the external enemy. This is how the right orientation is defined: 'Therefore, O Arjuna, surrendering all your works unto Me, with full knowledge of Me, without desires for profit, with no claims to proprietorship, and free from lethargy, fight' (3:30).

This demand for a lucid, supra-conscious heroism rising above the passions is important, as is this excerpt, which brings out the character of purity and absoluteness which action should have so as to be considered 'sacred war': 'Do thou fight for the sake of fighting, without considering happiness or distress, loss or gain, victory or defeat – and by so doing you shall never incur sin' (2:38).

We find therefore that the only fault or sin is the state of an incomplete will, of an action which, inwardly, is still far from the height from which one's own life matters as little as those of others and no human measure has value any longer.

---

3   From A. C. Bhaktivedanta Swami Prabhupada, *Bhagavad-Gita as It Is*. All quotes
    from the *Bhagavad-gita* are taken from this edition.

It is precisely in this respect that the text in question contains considerations of an absolutely metaphysical order, intended to show how that which acts in the warrior at such a level is not so much a human force as a divine force. The teaching which Krishna (that is to say the 'knowledge' principle) gives to Arjuna (that is to say to the 'action' principle) to make his doubts vanish aims, first of all, at making him understand the distinction between what, as absolute spirituality, is incorruptible, and what, as the human and naturalistic element, exists only illusorily: 'Those who are seers of the truth have concluded that of the non-existent [the material body] there is no endurance and of the eternal [the soul] there is no change. ... That which pervades the entire body you should know to be indestructible. No one is able to destroy that imperishable soul. ... Neither he who thinks the living entity the slayer nor he who thinks it slain is in knowledge, for the self slays not nor is slain. ... He is not slain when the body is slain. ... The material body of the indestructible, immeasurable and eternal living entity is sure to come to an end; therefore, fight...' (2:16, 17, 19, 20, 18).

But there is more. The consciousness of the metaphysical unreality of what one can lose or can cause another to lose, such as the ephemeral life and the mortal body – a consciousness which corresponds to the definition of human existence as 'a mere pastime' in one of the traditions which we have already considered – is associated with the idea that spirit, in its absoluteness and transcendence, can only appear as a destructive force towards everything which is limited and incapable of overcoming its own limited nature. Thus the problem arises of how the warrior can evoke the spirit, precisely in virtue of his being necessarily an instrument of destruction and death, and identify with it.

The answer to this problem is precisely what we find in our texts. The God not only declares, 'I am the strength of the strong, devoid of passion and desire. ... I am the original fragrance of the earth, and I am the heat in fire. I am the life of all that lives, and I am the penances of all ascetics. ... I am the original seed of all existences, the intelligence of the intelligent, and the prowess of all powerful men' (7:11, 9, 10), but, finally, the God reveals himself to Arjuna in the transcendent and fearful form of lightning. We thus arrive at this general vision of life: like electrical bulbs too brightly lit, like circuits invested with too high a potential, human beings fall and die only because a power burns within them which transcends their finitude, which goes beyond everything they can do and want. This is why they develop, reach a peak, and then, as if overwhelmed by the wave which up to a given point had carried them forward, sink, dissolve, die and return to the unmanifest. But the one who does not fear death, the one who is able, so to speak, to assume the powers of death by becoming everything which it destroys, overwhelms and shatters – this one finally passes beyond limitation, he continues to remain upon the crest of the wave, he does not fall, and what is beyond life manifests itself within him. Thus, Krishna, the personification of the 'principle of spirit', after having revealed himself fully to Arjuna, can say, 'With the exception of you, all the soldiers here on both sides will be slain. Therefore get up. Prepare to fight and win glory. Conquer your enemies and enjoy a flourishing kingdom. They are already put to death by My arrangement, and you, [O Arjuna], can be but an instrument in the fight. ... Therefore, kill them and do not be disturbed. Simply fight, and you will vanquish your enemies in battle' (32-34).

We see here again the identification of war with the 'path of God', of which we spoke in the previous article. The warrior ceases to act as a person. When he attains this level, a great non-human force transfigures his action, making it absolute and 'pure' precisely at its extreme. Here is a very evocative image belonging to the same tradition: 'Life – like a bow; the mind – like the arrow; the target to pierce – the supreme spirit; to join mind to spirit as the shot arrow hits its target.'

This is one of the highest forms of metaphysical justification of war, one of the most comprehensive images of war as 'sacred war'.

To conclude this excursion into the forms of heroic tradition, as presented to us by many different times and peoples, we will only add a few final words.

We have made this voyage into a world which, to some, could seem *outré*[4] and irrelevant, out of curiosity, not to display peculiar erudition. We have undertaken it instead with the precise intention of showing that the sacrality of war, that is to say, that which provides a spiritual justification for war and the necessity of war, constitutes a *tradition* in the highest sense of the term: it is something which has appeared always and everywhere, in the ascending cycle of every great civilisation; while the neurosis of war, the humanitarian and pacifist deprecation of it, as well as the conception of war as a 'sad necessity' or a purely political or natural phenomenon – *none of this corresponds to any tradition*. All this is but a modern fabrication, born yesterday, as a side-effect of the decomposition of the democratic and materialistic civilisation against which today new revolutionary forces are rising up. In this sense, everything which we have gathered from a great variety of sources, constantly separating the essential from the contingent, the spirit from the letter, can be used by us as an inner fortification, as a confirmation, as a strengthened certainty. Not only does a fundamentally virile instinct appear justified by it on a superior basis, but also the possibility presents itself of determining the forms of the heroic experience which correspond to our highest vocation.

Here we must refer to the first article of this series, in which we showed that there can be heroes of very different sorts, even of an animalistic and sub-personal sort; what matters is not merely the general capacity to throw oneself into combat and to sacrifice oneself, but also the precise *spirit* according to which such an event is experienced. But we now have all the elements needed to specify, from all the varied ways of understanding, the heroic experience, which may be considered the supreme one, and which can make the identification of war with the 'path of

---

4   French: 'to go to excess'.

God' really true, and can make one recognise, in the hero, a form of divine manifestation.

Another previous consideration must be recalled, namely, that as the warrior's vocation really approaches this metaphysical peak and reflects the impulse to what is universal, it cannot help but tend towards an equally universal manifestation and end for his race; that is to say, *it cannot but predestine that race for empire*. For only the empire as a superior order in which a *pax triumphalis*[5] is in force, almost as the earthly reflection of the sovereignty of the 'supra-world,' is adapted to forces in the field of spirit which reflect the great and free energies of nature, and are able to manifest the character of purity, power, irresistibility and transcendence over all pathos, passion and human limitation.

---

5   Latin: 'peace through victory'.

'Army' as Vision of the World[1]

U ndoubtedly, the new Fascist generation already possesses a broadly military, warlike orientation, but it has not yet grasped the necessity of integrating the details of simple discipline and psychophysical training into a superior order, a general vision of life.

The ethical aspect

One begins to see this when one studies our ancient traditions, which, certainly not by chance, so often used a symbolism taken from fighting, serving and asserting oneself heroically, to express purely spiritual realities. The group of initiates was called *stratos*, or 'army', in Orphism; *miles* expressed a degree of the Mithraic hierarchy; symbols of agony always recur in the sacred representations of classic Romanity, and passed, in part, to Christian asceticism itself.

But here we shall deal with something more precise than mere analogies, namely, the related doctrine of 'holy war', of which we have spoken previously in our books, as well as in these pages. We shall confine ourselves to the ethical field and refer to a special and central attitude, calculated to bring about a radical change of meaning in the whole field of values, and to raise it to a plane of

---

1   Originally published on 30 May 1937 as 'Sulla "Milizia" quale visione del mondo' in 'Diorama mensile', *Il Regime Fascista*.

manliness, separating it completely from all bourgeois attitudes, humanitarianism, moralism and limp conformism.

The basis of this attitude is summed up in Paul's well-known phrase, *vita est militia super terram*. It is a matter of conceiving the being here below as having been sent in the guise of a man on a mission of military service to a remote front, the purpose of this mission not always being directly sensed by the individual (in the same manner that one who fights in the outposts cannot always form a precise idea of the overall plan to which he contributes), but in which inner nobleness is always measured by the fact of resisting, of accomplishing, in spite of all, what must be accomplished, in the fact of not doubting, nor hesitating, in the fact of a fidelity stronger than life or death.

The first results of this view are an affirmative attitude with respect to the world: assertion and, at the same time, a certain freedom. He who is really a soldier is so by nature, and therefore because he wants to be so; in the missions and tasks which are given to him, consequently, he recognises himself, so to speak. Likewise, the one who conceives his existence as being that of a soldier in an army will be very far from considering the world as a vale of tears from which to flee, or as a circus of irrational events at which to throw himself blindly, or as a realm for which *carpe diem*[2] constitutes the supreme wisdom. Though he is not unaware of the tragic and negative side of so many things, his way of reacting to them will be quite different from that of all other men. His feeling that this world is not his Fatherland, and that it does not represent his proper condition, so to speak – his feeling that, basically, he 'comes from afar' – will remain a fundamental element which will not give rise to mystical escapism and spiritual weakness, but rather will enable him to minimise, to relativise, to refer to higher concepts of measure and limit, all that can seem important and definitive to others, starting with death itself, and will confer on him calm force and breadth of vision.

---

2 Latin: 'seize the day'.

The Social Aspect

The military conception of life, then, leads to a new sense of
social and political solidarity. It goes beyond all humanitarianism
and 'socialism': men are not our 'brothers', and our 'neighbour'
is in a way an insolent concept. Society is neither a creature of
necessity, nor something to be justified or sublimated on the basis
of the ideal of honeyed universal love and obligatory altruism.
Every society will instead be essentially conceived in the terms
of the solidarity existing between quite distinct beings, each one
determined to protect the dignity of its personality, but nevertheless united in a common action which binds them side by side,
without sentimentalism, in male comradeship. Fidelity and sincer-
ity, with the ethics of honour to which they give rise, will thus be
seen as the true basis of every community. According to ancient
Indo-Germanic legislation, killing did not appear to be as serious a fault as betrayal, or even mere lying. A warlike ethics would
also lead to more or less this attitude and it would be inclined to
limit the principle of solidarity by means of those of dignity and
affinity. The soldier can regard as comrades only those whom
he holds in esteem and who are resolute to hold to their posts,
not those who give way, the weak or the inept. Besides, the one
who guides has the duty of gathering and pushing forward the
valid forces, rather than wasting them on concern and lament
for those who have already fallen, or have yielded or have landed
themselves in *culs-de-sac*.

Sense of Stoicism

However, the views we put forward here are most valuable in terms
of inner strengthening. Here we enter in the field of a properly
Roman ethics, with which the reader should already be familiar
through those excerpts from classical authors which are published
on a regular basis in the 'Diorama'. As we have stated previously, we
speak here of an inner change, by virtue of which one's reactions
towards facts and life-experiences become absolutely different,
and, rather than being negative, as they are generally, become
positive and constructive. Stoic Romanity offers us an excellent

insight into this, provided that it is known as it really was, as true and indomitable life-affirmation, far from the preconceived opinions which endeavour to make us see in the Stoic only a stiffened, hardened being become foreign to life. Can one really doubt this, when Seneca[3] affirms the true man as superior to a god, since, while the latter is protected by nature from misfortune, man can meet the latter, challenge it, and show himself superior to it? Or when he calls unhappy those who have never been so, since they have never managed to know and to measure their force? In these authors precisely one can find many elements for a warlike system of ethics, which revolutionises completely the common manner of thinking. A very characteristic aspect of this viewpoint is this: the one who is sent off to a dangerous place curses his fate only if he is a vile person; if he is a heroic spirit, he is instead proud of it, since he knows that his commander chooses the worthiest and strongest for any risky mission and for any post of responsibility, leaving the most convenient and secure posts only to those whom he basically does not hold in esteem.

This same thought is appropriate to the most dark, tragic, discouraging moments of life: it is necessary to discover in these either a hidden providentiality or an appeal to our nobility and superiority.

'Who is worthy of the name of Man, and of Roman', Seneca writes precisely, 'who does not want to be tested and does not look for a dangerous task? For the strong man inaction is torture. There is only one sight able to command the attention even of a god, and it is that of a strong man battling with bad luck, especially if he has himself challenged it.'

This is a wisdom, besides, which is taken from ancient ages, and finds a place even in a general conception of the history of the world. If Hesiod, before the spectacle of the Age of Iron, the dark and deconsecrated age which is identified as the last age, exclaimed, 'If only then I did not have to live [in the Age of

---

3   Seneca (4 BC-65 AD) was a noted Roman writer and philosopher. He committed suicide after being accused of involvement in an assassination plot against the Emperor Nero.

Iron], but could have either died first or been born afterwards!',[4] a teaching peculiar to the ancient Indo-Germanic traditions was that precisely those who, in the dark age, resist in spite of all will be able to obtain fruits which those who lived in more favourable, less hard, periods could seldom reach.

Thus the vision of one's life as membership within an army gives shape to an ethic of its own and to a precise inner attitude which arouses deep forces. On this basis, to seek membership in an actual army, with its disciplines and its readiness for absolute action on the plane of material struggle, is the right direction and the path which must be followed. It is necessary to first feel oneself to be a soldier in spirit and to render one's sensibility in accordance with that in order to be able to do this also in a material sense subsequently, and to avoid the dangers which, in the sense of a materialistic hardening and overemphasis on the purely physical, can otherwise come from militarisation on the external plane alone: whereas, given this preparation, any external form can easily become the symbol and instrument of properly spiritual meanings.

A Fascist system of ethics, if thought through thoroughly, cannot but be directed along those lines. 'Scorn for the easy life' is the starting point. The further points of reference must still be placed as high as possible, beyond everything which can speak only to feeling and beyond all mere myth.

If the two most recent phases of the involutionary process which has led to the modern decline are first, the rise of the bourgeoise, and second, the collectivisation not only of the idea of the State, but also of all values and of the conception of ethics itself, then to go beyond all this and to reassert a 'warlike' vision of life in the aforementioned full sense must constitute the pre-condition for any reconstruction: when the world of the masses and of the materialistic and sentimental middle classes gives way to a world of 'warriors', the main thing will have been achieved, which makes possible the coming of an even higher order, that of true traditional spirituality.

---

4   Hesiod, *Theogony* (Cambridge: Harvard University Press/The Loeb Classical Library, 2006), pp. 101-102.

Race and War[1]

One of the most serious obstacles to a purely biological formulation of the doctrine of race is the fact that cross-breeding and contamination of the blood are not the only cause of the decline and decay of races. Races may equally degenerate and come to their end because of a process – so to speak – of inner extinction, without the participation of external factors. In purely biological terms this may correspond to those enigmatic 'inner variations' (idiovariations) which science has been forced to recognise are just as powerful as variations due to cross-breeding in bringing about mutations.

This will never be completely understood if the biological conception of race is not integrated with that 'racism of the second and of the third degree' of which we have repeatedly spoken here. It is only if race is considered as existing not only in the body, but also in the soul and in the spirit, as a deep, meta-biological force which conditions both the physical and the psychical structures in the organic totality of the human entity – it is only if this eminently traditional point of view is assumed – that the mystery of the decline of races can be fathomed in all its aspects. One can then realise that, in a way analogous to the individual abdication and inner breakdown of the individual, where the loss of all moral tension and the attitude of passive abandonment can gradually

1   Originally published on 20 October 1939 as 'La razza e la guerra' in *La Difesa della Razza*.

find expression in a true physical collapse, or can paralyse natural organic resources far more efficiently than any threat to the body – so developments of the same nature can occur on the plane of those greater entities which are human races, on the greater scale in space and in time of their aggregate life spans. And what we have just pointed out about organic resources neutralised, when the inner – moral and spiritual – tension of an individual is lacking, can even allow us to consider less simplistically and less materialistically the matter of racial alterations due to mixing and contamination, as well.

This is quite similar to what happens in infections. It is known, in fact, that bacteria and microbes are not always the sole effective and unilateral causes of illness: for a disease to be acquired by contagion a certain more or less strong predisposition is necessary. The state of integrity or tonicity of the organism, in turn, conditions this predisposition, and this is greatly affected by the spiritual factor, the presence of the whole being to himself, and his state of inner intrepidity or anguish. In accordance with this analogy, we may believe that, for cross-breeding to have a really, fatally, inexorably degenerative outcome for a race, it is necessary without exception that this race already be damaged inwardly to a certain extent, and that the tension of its original will be lax as a result.

When a race has been reduced to a mere ensemble of atavistic automatisms, which have become the sole surviving vestiges of what it once was, then a collision, a lesion, a simple action from outside, is enough to make it fall, to disfigure it and to denature it. In such a case, it does not behave like an elastic body, ready to react and to resume its original shape after the collision (provided, that is, that the latter does not exceed certain limits and does not produce permanent actual damage), but, rather, it behaves like a rigid, inelastic body, which passively endures the imprint of external action.

On the basis of these considerations two practical tasks of racism can be distinguished. The first task could be said to be one of passive defence. This means sheltering the race from all external actions (crossings, unsuitable forms of life and culture, etc.) which could present the danger to it of a crisis, a mutation or a denaturation. The second task, in contrast, is active resistance, and consists in reducing to a minimum the predisposition of the race to degeneration, that is to say, the ground on which it can be exposed passively to external action. This means, essentially, 'to exalt' its inner race; to see to it that its intimate tension is never lacking; that, as a counterpart of its physical integrity, within it there is something like an uncontrollable and irreducible fire, always yearning for new material to feed its blaze, in the form of new obstacles, which defy it and force it to reassert itself.

This second task is obviously more arduous than the first, because it can demand solutions which vary from individual to individual, and because external, general and material measures are of little use for it. It is a matter of overcoming the inertia of spirit, that force of gravity which is in force in human interiority no less than in the outer, physical world, and here finds expression precisely in the inclination to abandonment, to 'take it easy', to always follow the path of least resistance. But, unfortunately, for the individual as well as for the race, to overcome this danger it is necessary to have a support – for the ability to act directly, to always remain at the crest of the wave, to maintain an inner initiative which is always renewed, without the need for renewed stimuli, can only occur as the result of an exceptional endowment, and cannot reasonably be demanded as a matter of course. As we have said, for tension which has become latent to reawaken before it is too late and the processes of the automatisation of race follow, an obstacle, a test, almost a challenge, is necessary. It is then that the crisis and the decision occur: by their way of reacting, the deeper, meta-biological powers of the race then show whether they have remained stronger than the contingencies and the destinies of the given period of history. In the case of a positive reaction, new potentialities come from deep inside to again saturate the racial circuit. A new ascending cycle begins for that race.

In some cases, it is even possible that precision cross-breeding – naturally kept within very stringent limits – carries out a function of that kind. This is well-known in zootechnics. The 'pure breed' in some animal species is both the result of the preservation of heredity and of judicious cross-breeding. We do not share the opinion of Chamberlain,[2] who was inclined to apply this kind of thinking to the 'superior races' of humanity. However, it is a well-proven fact that in some aristocratic families, which, with their centuries-old blood law, have been the only experimental field for racism in history so far, some cross-breedings have had precisely the merit of preventing extinction of the line through inner degeneration. Here – let us stress – the cross-breeding has the function of an ordeal, not a rule – an ordeal, moreover, which can also present a dangerous challenge for the blood. But danger reawakens the spirit. Before the heterogeneous element introduced by cross-breeding, the homogenous nucleus is called to reaffirm itself, to assimilate to himself what is alien, to act towards it in the capacity of the 'dominant' towards the 'recessive', in terms of the Laws of Mendel.[3] If the reaction is positive, the result is an awakening. The stock which seemed spent and exhausted reawakens. But if it has already fallen too much, or if the heterogeneity is excessive, the ordeal fails and the decline is quick and definitive.

But the highest instrument of the inner awakening of race is combat, and war is its highest expression. That pacifism and humanitarianism are phenomena closely linked to internationalism, democracy, cosmopolitanism and liberalism is perfectly logical – the same anti-racial instinct present in some is reflected and confirmed in the others. The will towards sub-racial levelling inborn in internationalism finds its ally in pacifist humanitarianism, which has the function of preventing the heroic test from disrupting the game by galvanising the surviving forces of any remaining not completely deracinated peoples. It is odd, however, and illustrates the errors to which a unilaterally biological formu-

---

2   Houston Stewart Chamberlain (1855-1927) was one of the most influential racial theorists of the early Twentieth century. His most important work was *The Foundations of the Nineteenth Century* (New York: John Lane, 1910).

3   Gregor Johann Mendel (1822-1884) was a Czech-German scientist, and is often called 'the father of modern genetics'. Mendel's Laws of Inheritance, based on his study of plants across several generations, attempted to define how specific characteristics are transmitted from parents to their offspring.

lation of the racial problem can lead, that the racial theory of 'mis-selections', as expressed for example by Vacher de Lapouge,[4] partakes, to a certain extent, of the same incomprehension of the positive meaning of war for race – but here, in the face of full knowledge of the facts – as is found in internationalist democratism. To be specific, they suppose that every war turns into a progressive elimination of the best, of the exponents of the still-pure race of the various peoples, thus facilitating an involution.

This is a partial view, because it only considers what is lost through the disappearance of some individuals, not what is aroused to a much greater extent in others by the experience of war, which otherwise would never have been aroused. This becomes even more obvious if we do not consider ancient wars which were largely fought by elites while the lower strata were spared by them, but rather modern wars which engage entire armed nations and which, moreover, in their character of totality, involve not only physical but also moral and spiritual forces of combatants and non-combatants alike. The Jew Ludwig[5] expressed fury about an article published in a German military review which brought out the possibilities of selection related to air bombardments, in which the test of sang-froid, the immediate, lucid reaction of the instinct of direction in opposition to brutal or confused impulse, cannot but result in a decisive discrimination of those who have the greatest probability of escaping and surviving from those who do not.

The indignation of the humanitarian Jew Ludwig, who has become the bellicose propagator of the 'new Holy Alliance' against fascism, is powerless against what is truthful in considerations of this sort. If the next world war is a 'total war' it will also

---

4   Georges Vacher de Lapouge (1854-1936) was a French anthropologist, socialist, and racial theorist. He was the author of *L'Aryen: son rôle social* (*The Aryan and His Social Role*), published in Paris in 1899 and never translated into English. In this work he classified the various races, and proposed that the European Aryans are in opposition to the Jews as racial archetypes. His ideas were highly influential upon the racialist and eugenics movements.

5   Emil Ludwig (1881-1948) was primarily known at the time as the author of a number of popular biographies of historical figures, including Goethe, Bismarck and Mussolini.

mean a 'total test' of the surviving racial forces of the modern
world. Without doubt, some will collapse, whereas others will
awake and rise. Nameless catastrophes could even be the hard but
necessary price of heroic peaks and new liberations of primordial
forces dulled through grey centuries. But such is the fatal condition for the creation of any new world – and it is a new world
that we seek for the future.

What we have said here must be considered as a mere introduction to the question of the significance which war has, in
general, for race. Three fundamental points should be considered
in conclusion. First, since we proceed from the assumption that
there is a fundamental difference between human races – a difference which, according to the doctrine of the three degrees of
racism,[6] is not restricted to corporeality but concerns also soul
and spirit – it should be expected that the spiritual and physical
behaviour towards the experience or test of war varies between
the various races; it will therefore be both necessary and interesting to define the sense according to which, for each specific race,
the aforementioned reaction will occur.

Second, it is necessary to consider the interdependent relationship between what a well-understood racial policy can do to
promote the aims of war, and, conversely, what war, in the presupposition of a correct spiritual attitude, can do to promote the
aims of race. We can speak, in this respect, of a sort of germ, or
primary nucleus, created initially or reawakened by racial policy,
which brings out racial values in the consciousness of a people;
a germ or nucleus which will bear fruit by giving the war a value,
while conversely the experience of war, and the instincts and cur-
rents of deep forces which emerge through such an experience,
give the racial sense a correct, fecund direction.

And this leads us to the third and last point. People are accus-
tomed to speaking too generally, and too romantically, about
'heroism', 'heroic experience' and the like. When they are done

---

6   For more on Evola's theory of race, see 'Julius Evola's Concept of Race: A Racism
    of Three Degrees' by Michael Bell at *Counter-Currents*, www.counter-currents.
    com/2011/02/julius-evolas-concept-of-race/. Available as of 26 April 2011.

with such romantic assumptions, in modern times, there seem to remain only material ones, such that men who rise up and fight are considered simply as 'human material', and the heroism of the combatants is related to victory as merely a means to an end, the end itself being nothing but the increase of the material and economic power and territory of a given state.

In view of the considerations which have been pointed out here, it is necessary to change these attitudes. From the 'ordeal by fire' of the primordial forces of race and heroic experience, above all other experience, has been a means to an essentially spiritual and interior end. But there is more: heroic experience differentiates itself in its results not only according to the various races, but also according to the extent to which, within each race, a super-race has formed itself and come to power. The various degrees of this creative differentiation correspond to so many ways of being a hero and to so many forms of awakening through heroic experience. On the lowest plane, hybrid, essentially vital, instinctive and collective forces emerge – this is somewhat similar to the awakening on a large scale of the 'primordial horde' by the solidarity, unity of destiny and holocaust which is peculiar to it. Gradually, this mostly naturalistic experience is purified, dignified, and becomes luminous until it reaches its highest form, which corresponds to the Aryan conception of war as 'holy war', and of victory and triumph as an apex, since its value is identical to the values of holiness and initiation, and, finally, of death on the battlefield as *mors triumphalis*, as not a rhetorical but an effective overcoming of death.

Having indicated all these points in a basic but, we trust, sufficiently intelligible manner, we propose to tackle them one by one in writings which will follow the present one, each of which will specifically consider the varieties of heroic experience according to race and then the vision of war peculiar to the Nordic-Aryan and Ario-Roman tradition in particular.

Two Heroisms[1]

To pursue our previous discussions about the varied meanings that the fact of war and the experience of heroism can represent for the race it is necessary to briefly explain the concept of the 'super-race' and the related distinction between races as given by 'nature' and races in the higher, human and spiritual sense.

According to the traditional view, man as such is not reducible to purely biological, instinctive, hereditary, naturalistic determinisms; if all this has its part, which is wrongly neglected by a spiritualism of dubious value, the fact still remains that man distinguishes himself from the animal insofar as he participates also in a super-natural, super-biological element, solely in accordance with which he can be free and be himself. Generally, these two aspects of the human being are not necessarily in contradiction with one another. Although it obeys its own laws, which must be respected, that which in man is 'nature' allows itself to be the organ and instrument of expression and action of that in him which is more than 'nature'. It is only in the vision of life peculiar to Semitic peoples, and above all to the Jewish people, that corporeality becomes 'flesh', as root of every sin, and irreducible antagonist of spirit.

We should apply this way of seeing the individual to these vaster individualities which are races. Some races can be compared

---

1   Originally published on 20 November 1939 as 'Due eroismi' in *La Difesa della Razza*.

to the animal, or to the man who, degrading himself, has passed
to a purely animalistic way of life: such are the 'races of nature'.
They are not illuminated by any superior element; no force from
above supports them in the vicissitudes and contingencies with
which their life in space and in time presents them. In these
ordeals, what predominates in them is the collectivist element, in
the form of instinct, 'genius of the species', or spirit and unity
of the horde. Broadly speaking, the feeling of race and blood
here can be stronger and surer than in other peoples or stocks:
nevertheless, it always represents something sub-personal and
completely naturalistic, such as, for example, the dark 'totemism'
of savage populations, in which the totem, which is in a way the
mystical entity of the race or tribe but meaningfully associated
with a given animal species, is conceived as something prior to
each individual, as soul of its soul, not in the abstract, in theory,
but in every expression of daily life. Having referred to the savages, incidentally, and reserving the right to return eventually to
the argument involved, we must indicate the error of those who
consider the savages as 'primitives', that is, as the original forms of
humanity; from which, according to the usual mendacious theory
of the inferior miraculously giving rise to the superior, superior
races would have 'evolved'. In many cases it is exactly the contrary
which is true. Savages, and many races which we can consider as
'natural', are only the last degenerate remnants of vanished, far
anterior, superior races and civilisations, even the name of which
has often not reached us. This is why the presumed 'primitives'
who still exist today do not tend to 'evolve', but rather disappear
definitively and become extinct.

In other races, however, the naturalistic element is, so to speak,
the vehicle of a superior, super-biological element, which is to
the former what the spirit is to the body. Such an element almost
always becomes incarnated in the tradition of such races and in
the elite which embodies this tradition and keeps it alive. Here,
therefore, there is a race of the spirit behind the race of body
and blood in which the latter expresses the former in a more or

less perfect manner according to the circumstances, individuals, and often castes, in which this race is articulated.

The truth of this is clearly felt wherever, in symbolic form, Antiquity attributed 'divine' or 'celestial' origins to a given race or caste. In this context, therefore, purity of blood, or the lack of it, is no longer sufficient to define the essence and rank of a given race. Where the regime of the castes was in force every caste could obviously be considered 'pure' because the law of endogamy or non-mixing applied to all of them. Not to have merely pure blood, but to have – symbolically – 'divine' blood, instead defined the superior caste or race with respect to the plebeian one, or to what we have called the 'race of nature'. Hence the fact that, in the ancient Indo-Germanic civilisations of the East, the community or spiritual race of the *âryâ* identified itself with that of the *dvîja*, the 'twice-born' or 'reborn': this was a reference to a supernatural element pertaining to it, to latent gifts of 'race' in a superior sense, which a special ritual, compared to a second birth or to a regeneration, had to progressively confirm in the individual. But maybe we will have to go back over this also; these points are, however, sufficient for the argument which we now intend to make.

We need only add that, if we look at humanity today, not only is it difficult to find a group which maintains one race of the body or another in the pure state, but it should unfortunately also be recognised that the general distinction between naturalistic races and superior races, or super-races, becomes in very many cases extremely uncertain: often, modern man has lost both the steadiness of instinct of the 'races of nature' and the superiority and metaphysical tension of the 'super-race'. He looks rather like what primitive peoples in reality, and not in the view of evolutionists, are: beings which, even though they proceed from originally superior races, have degraded themselves to animalistic, naturalistic, amorphous and semi-collectivist ways of life. What Landra[2] has accurately described in these pages as 'the race of the bourgeois', of the petty conformist and right-thinking man,

---

2   Guido Landra was an anthropologist, and was the first director of the Office of
    Racial Studies, a department within the Ministry of Popular Culture of Fascist Italy.

the 'advanced' spirit who invents a superiority for himself on the basis of rhetoric, empty speculations and exquisite aestheticisms; the pacifist, the social climber, the neutralist humanitarian, all this half-extinguished material of which so significant a part of the modern world is made up, is actually a product of racial degeneration, the expression of the deep crisis of the Man of the West, all the more tragic as it is not even felt as such.

Let us now come to the fact of war and the experience of heroism. Both, we have claimed in our previous writings, are instruments of awakening. An awakening, however, of what? War, experienced, determines a first selection; it separates the strong from the weak, the heroes from the cowards. Some fall, others assert themselves. But this is not enough. Various ways of being heroes, various meanings, can arise in heroic experience. From each race, a different, specific reaction must be expected. Let us ignore this fact for now and follow instead the 'phenomenology' of the awakening of race determined by war, that is, the various typical modalities of this awakening, working theoretically on the distinction which has just been made ('race of nature' and 'super-race') and practically on the concrete aspect, that is to say the fact that, since it is no longer specialised warlike elites but masses which face war, war therefore to a great extent concerns the mixed, bourgeois, half-degraded type, whom we have described above as a product of crisis.

To put such a product of crisis to the test of fire, to impose upon him a fundamental alternative, not theoretical, but in terms of reality and even of life and death: this is the first healthy effect of the fact of war for race. *Ignis essentiae*, in the terminology of ancient alchemists: the fire which tests, which strips to the 'essence'.

To follow this development more concretely we shall refer to the unique documentation which is found in famous authors such as, for example, Erich Maria Remarque and the French René Quinton.[3]

---

3   René Quinton (1866-1925) was the author of *Soldier's Testament: Selected Maxims of René Quinton* (London: Eyre & Spottiswoode, 1930). This is the English version of the book discussed by Evola below.

Everyone knows Remarque as the author of the notorious novel *All Quiet on the Western Front,*[4] considered a masterpiece of defeatism. Our opinion in this matter is no different: it is nevertheless worth examining this novel with the coldest objectivity. The characters of the novel are teenagers who were imbued as volunteers with every sort of 'idealism', resonant with that rhetorical, romantic and choreographically heroic conception of war spread by those people who, with fanfare and beautiful speeches, had limited themselves to accompanying them to the station. Once they have reached the front and have been caught in the true experience of modern war, they come to realise that it is something quite different and that none of the ideals and the aforementioned rhetoric can support them any longer. They do not become either vile wretches or traitors, but their inner being is transformed; it is an irremediably broken generation, even where the howitzers have spared it. They advance, they often become 'heroes' – but as what? They feel war to be an elemental, impersonal, inhuman vicissitude, a vicissitude of unleashed forces, in which to survive is only possible by reawakening as beings made of instincts which are absolute, as lucid as they are inexorable, instincts almost independent from their persons. These are the forces which carry such youngsters forward, which lead them to assert themselves where others would have been broken, or would have been driven crazy, or would have preferred the fate of the deserters and the vile wretches: but, beyond this, no enthusiasm, no ideal, no light. To mark in a morbidly evocative manner the terrible anonymity of this vicissitude, in which the individual no longer counts, Remarque makes the book end with the death of the only young person in the original group who had escaped, and who dies almost at the threshold of the armistice, on a day so calm that the communiqués confine themselves to this sentence: 'All quiet on the western front'.

Even leaving aside the fact that the author of this book actually was a combatant, it would be hard to say that processes of this sort

---

4   *All Quiet on the Western Front* (Boston: Little, Brown & Co., 1929). It is perhaps the most famous anti-war novel ever written.

are only 'novelistic', without relation to reality. The defeatism of the book, its insidious and deleterious side, lies rather in reducing the whole war, that is, all the possibilities of the experience of war, to a single, certainly real, but particular, aspect of it; in fact this is merely the negative outcome of a test, which, however, can be overcome by others positively. A point should be borne in mind: the anti-bourgeois thesis. Up to this point, we can even agree with Remarque. War acts as a catharsis, as a 'purification': *ignis essentiae*. Beautiful words, beautiful feelings, rhetorical flights, myths and watchwords, humanitarianism and verbose patriotism are swept away, and so is the petty person with the illusion of its importance and its usefulness. All this is far too little. One is in the face of pure forces. And, to resist, one must reawaken likewise as an embodiment of pure forces intimately connected with the depth of race: forgetting one's own 'I', one's own life. But it is precisely here that the two opposite possibilities show themselves: once the superstructures of the 'race of limbo', of the bourgeois, half-extinguished man, have been blown up, two ways of overcoming the 'human' are likewise open: the shift to the sub-human, or the shift to the super-human. In one case, the beast reawakens; in the other, the hero in the true sense, the sacred and traditional sense; in the former, the 'race of nature' revives, and, in the latter, the 'super-race'. Remarque only knows the first solution.

Some years ago, a work by René Quinton was published in Italian translation: *Massime sulla guerra*. It represents another very singular testimony. Eight times injured in the World War, repeatedly decorated with the most coveted decorations, Quinton can obviously aspire to the generic qualification of 'hero'. But what meaning has this 'hero' experienced in war? This book is the answer. War is conceived and justified by Quinton biologically, in close dependency on the instincts of the species and 'natural selection'. Some quotations:

> There are, at the base of any being, two motives:
> the egoistic one which drives him to conserve

his own life, and the altruistic one which leads him to forget himself, to sacrifice himself for a natural end which he does not know and which becomes identified with the benefit of the species. Thus, the weak, in the service of the species, attacks the more powerful, without prudence, without reason, without even hoping to win. The genius of the species commands him to attack and to gamble his life [...] The male and the female are created for the service of the species. The males are organised to fight each other [for the purpose of sexual selection]. War is their natural state, as for the female the sacred order is to conceive and then to nurture.

Hence this singular conception of heroism:

> The hero does not act from a sense of duty, but from love [meaning: according to race instincts, which the sexual function obeys]. In war man is no longer man, he is only the male [...] War is a chapter of love – males become intoxicated with tearing each other to pieces. The drunkenness of war is a drunkenness of love.

The instrument of the species, of the race of the body, in a primordial outburst, according to Quinton:

> Thus, there is nothing sublime about the hero, nor about the heroic mother who rushes towards a fire in order to save her child: they are the born male and female.

To indicate the conclusion that all this leads to, we will quote these further excerpts from Quinton:

> Every ideal is a pretext to kill. Hatred is the most important thing in life. The wise men who no longer hate are ready for sterility and death. You must not understand the [enemy] peoples, you must hate them. The more man rises, the more his hatred for man grows. Nature has by no means created males, and peoples, in order for them to love each other.

The joy of hurting the adversary constitutes, then, one of the essential elements of the hero.

> Socialised life is composed of merely artificial duties. War frees man from these and returns him to his primal instincts.

In the evolutionistic-biological framework of a view such as this, these instincts are essentially dependent on race, in the sense of species.

Just as it would be inaccurate to regard Remarque merely as a jaundiced defeatist, so it would be inaccurate to regard Quinton merely as a combatant who, in trying to express his experiences theoretically, became a victim of the notorious theory of combat as the natural selection of the species. There is more. There is, despite several features of caricature and one-sidedness, a sign of real life. Actually, the lion can arise from the sheep precisely in this sense. Man reawakens and resumes contact with the deep forces of life and race from which he had become alienated, but in order to be no more than a 'male' and, at best, a "magnificent beast of prey". In the realm of the 'races of nature', this may be normal, and the phenomena by which experiences of that sort are likely to be accompanied – horde solidarity, unity of destiny, etc. – may even have a healthy, reviving effect for a given organised ethnic group. But from the point of view of one who already belongs to a 'race of the spirit' this can only be his ordeal of fire turned into a fall. The catharsis, the amputation of the 'bourgeois' excrescence brought about by war, here, exposes not what is superior to the ideal of personality but what is inferior to it, marking the borderline point of the involution of the race of the spirit into that of the body. To use the terms of ancient Aryan traditions, this is *pitr-yâna*, the path of those who are dissolved in dark ancestral forces, not *dêva-yâna*, the 'path of gods'.[5]

Let us now consider the other possibility, that is, the case in which the experience of war turns into a restoration, an awakening, of the race of the spirit, or 'super-race'. We have already stated the normal relationship in the super-race between the biological element and the super-biological one, or, if we prefer, between the 'vital' element and the properly spiritual one. The former must be considered as an instrument for the manifestation and expression of the latter. Having this point of reference, the essentials of the positive solution can be expressed in a very simple formula: heroic experience and, in general, the experience of risk, of combat, of painful tension, must constitute for the individual one of those inner culminations in which the extreme intensity of life (*quâ*[6] biological element) is almost transformed into something more-than-life (the supra-biological element). This implies a freeing upwards from the confines of individuality and the assumption of the bursting upwards of the deeper side of one's own being as the instrument of a sort of active ecstasy, implying not the deepening but the transfiguration of personality, and, with it, of all lucid vision, precise action, command and domination. Such moments, such culminations of heroic experience, not only do not exclude, but actually demand all the aspects of war that have an 'elemental', destructive, we could almost say telluric, character: precisely that which, in the eyes of the petty individuality and the petty 'I', the unwarlike 'intellectual' and the

---

5   This is discussed in the Upanisads, especially *Brhadaranyaka Upanisad*.

6   Latin: 'by virtue of being'.

sentimental humanitarian, has a baleful, deplorable, deleterious character for 'human values', and shows itself instead here to have spiritual value. Even death – death on the battlefield – becomes, in this respect, a testimony to life; hence the Roman conception of the *mors triumphalis* and the Nordic conception of Valhalla as a place of immortality exclusively reserved for 'heroes'. But there is more: the assumptions of such heroic experience seem to possess an almost magical effectiveness: they are inner triumphs which can determine even material victory and are a sort of evocation of divine forces intimately tied to 'tradition' and the 'race of the spirit' of a given stock. That is why, in the ritual of the triumph in Rome, the victorious leader bore the insignia of the Capitoline divinity.

These remarks are sufficient to allow the reader to anticipate that what we say is not a mere 'theory' of ours, a philosophical position or interpretation thought up by us. This doctrine of heroism as a sacred and almost magical culmination, this mystical and ascetic conception of fighting and of winning, itself expresses a precise tradition, today forgotten but extensively documented in the testimonies of ancient civilisations, and especially of Aryan ones. This is why, in a subsequent article, we propose to express the same meanings by making ancient myths and symbols and rituals, Roman and Indo-Germanic, speak, which will clarify what, so far, we have had necessarily to expose in a synthetic and general form.

Race and War: The Aryan Conception of Combat[1]

In our previous article, dealing with the capacity of war and heroic experience to bring about an awakening of deep forces connected to the substratum of the race, we have seen that, in the most general way, two distinct, and indeed opposite, types appear. In the first type, the petty bourgeois personality – tamed, conformist, pseudo-intellectual or emptily idealistic – may undergo a disintegration, involving the emergence of elementary forces and instincts, in which the individual regresses to the pre-personal stage of the 'races of nature', which exhaust themselves in a welter of conservative and affirmative instincts. In the second type, in contrast, the most 'elemental' and non-human aspects of the heroic experience become a means of transfiguration, of elevation and integration of personality in – so to speak – a transcendent way of being. This constitutes an evocation of what we have called 'the race of the spirit', that is, of the spiritual element from 'above', which, in superior stocks, acts formatively on the purely biological part, and is at the root of their 'tradition' and of their prophetic greatness – simultaneously, from the point of view of the individual, these are experiences which Antiquity, and specifically Aryan antiquity, considered no

---

1   Originally published on 20 December 1939 as 'La razza e la guerra: la concezione ariana del combattere' in *La Difesa della Razza*.

less rich in supernatural fruits than those of asceticism, holiness and even initiation. Having thus recalled our point of departure, let us specify the subjects which we intend to develop further. First of all, as we have said, we want to present a brief account which makes it apparent that the aforementioned conception of heroism, far from being the product of a particular speculation of ours, or of an empty rhetorical projection, corresponds to a precise tradition which appears in a whole series of ancient civilisations. In the second place, we want to develop the Aryan conception of 'victory', understood precisely as a 'mystical' value, closely connected to an inner rebirth. Finally, passing to a more concrete plane, we want to see, in general terms, of what is the behaviour of the various races in relation to this order of ideas. In the present article, we will deal thoroughly with the first point.

Broadly speaking, we find that, especially among ancient Aryan humanity, wars were thought of as images of a perennial fight between metaphysical forces: on one hand there was the Olympian and luminous principle, uranic and solar truth; on the other hand there was raw force, the 'titanic', telluric element, 'barbaric' in the classical sense, the demonic-feminine principle of chaos. This view continually recurs in Greek mythology in various symbolic forms; in still more precise and radical terms it appears in the general vision of the world of the Irano-Aryan races, which considered themselves literally to be the armies of the God of Light in his struggle against the power of darkness; they persist throughout the Middle Ages, often retaining their classical features in spite of the new religion. Thus, Frederick I of Swabia,[2] in his fight against the rebellious Commune, recalled the symbol of Hercules and the arm with which this symbolic hero of Dorian-Aryan and Achaean-Aryan stocks fought as all of the 'Olympian' forces against the dark creatures of chaos.

This general conception, intimately experienced, could not help but be reflected in more concrete forms of life and activity,

---

2   Frederick I (1122-1190), also known as Barbarossa (Redbeard), was the Holy Roman Emperor. He led six invasions of Italy, and was a Crusader. According to legend, he was also one of the holders of the Spear of Destiny (the Lance which pierced the side of Christ), and will one day return to restore Germany to its former greatness.

raised to the symbolic and, we could almost say, 'ritual-like' level. For our purposes, it is worth noting particularly the transformation of war into the 'path of God' and 'greater holy war'.

We omit deliberately here any documentation peculiar to Romanity because we will use this when dealing, in the next article, with the 'mysticism of victory'. We will begin instead with the testimonies, which are themselves very well-known, relating to the Nordic-Aryan tradition. Here, Valhalla is the place of an immortality reserved above all for heroes fallen on the battlefield. The Lord of this place, Odin or Wotan, is presented to us in the *Ynglingasaga* as having shown to the heroes, by his own symbolic self-sacrifice on the cosmic tree Yggdrasil, the path which leads to that divine sojourn, where they live eternally, as if on a dazzling luminous peak beyond the clouds.

According to this tradition, no sacrifice or cult is more appreciated by the supreme God than that which is performed by the hero who fights and falls on the battlefield. In addition to this there is a sort of metaphysical counterpart reinforcing this view: the forces of the heroes who, having fallen and sacrificed themselves to Odin, have gone beyond the limits of human nature, and then increase the phalanx which this god needs to fight the *Ragna-rökkr*, that is, the 'darkening of the divine', which has threatened the world since ancient times. In the *Edda*, in fact, it is said that 'no matter how great the number of the heroes gathered in Valhalla, they will never be too many for when the Wolf comes'. The 'Wolf' here is the symbol of a dark and wild power which, previously, had managed to chain and subdue the stock of the 'divine heroes', or Aesir; the 'age of the Wolf'[3] is more or less the counterpart of the 'Age of Iron' in the Classical tradition, and of the 'dark age' – Kali-Yuga[4] – in the Indo-Aryan one: it alludes

---

3   The Age of the Wolf is described in the 45th verse of the 'Völuspá', or Prophecy of the Seeress, the first poem of the Norse *Poetic Edda*. The wolf age is said to be the age of brother turning against brother, constant warfare, widespread whoredom and hardship. It is the prelude to the end of the world, although the world is destined to be recreated afterward in an even more perfect form. See *The Poetic Edda* (Oxford: Oxford University Press, 1996).

4   The last and darkest age in the Vedic, or Hindu, cycle of ages.

symbolically to an age of the unleashing of purely terrestrial and desecrated forces.

It is important to note that similar meanings remain under the Christian outer garment in the Medieval ideology of the Crusades. The liberation of the Temple and the conquest of the Holy Land had a much closer relationship than is commonly supposed with ancient traditions relating to mystical Asgard, a distant land of heroes, where there is no death, and whose inhabitants enjoy an incorruptible life and supernatural calm. 'Holy war' appeared as a very spiritual war, so much so that it could be compared literally by ancient chroniclers to 'a bathing, which is almost like the fire of purgatory before death' – a clear reference to the ascetic meaning of combat. 'It is a glory for you never to leave the battle [unless] covered with laurels. But it is an even greater glory to earn on the battlefield an immortal crown ...' said Saint Bernard to the Crusaders, addressing especially the Templars, in his *De Laude Novae Militiae*.[5] *Glorie asolue*,[6] attributed to the Lord who is above, in the skies – *in excelsis Deo* – was promised to the warrior in Provençal texts.

Moreover, the first military setbacks undergone by the Crusaders, which were initially a source of surprise and dismay, served to purify the notion of war from any residue of materialism and superstitious devotion. The unhappy fate of a crusade was compared by the Pope and the **clerks** to that of an unfortunate life, which is judged and rewarded only according to the criteria of a non-earthly life and justice. Thus, the Crusaders learned to regard something as superior to victory and defeat, and to regard all value as residing in the spiritual aspect of action.

Thus we approach the most inward aspect of heroic experience, its ascetic value: it should not cause surprise if, to characterise it further, we now turn to the Muslim tradition, which might seem to be the opposite pole to the one just discussed. The truth is that the races which confronted each other in the Crusades were both warlike ones, which experienced in war the

---

5   *In Praise of the New Knighthood* (Piscataway: Gorgias Press, 2010).

6   Latin: 'absolute glory'.

same supra-material meaning, even while fighting against one other. In any case, the ideas which we wish to discuss now are essentially to be considered as echoes within the Muslim tradition of an originally Persian (Aryo-Iranian) conception, assumed now by members of the Arab race.

In the Muslim tradition, in fact, we find the central nucleus of the whole order of ideas dealt with here in the theory of the twofold war, that is, of the 'lesser and greater *jihad*'. The lesser war is the material war fought against a hostile people and, in particular, against an unjust one, the 'barbarians' or 'infidels', in which case it becomes the 'lesser *jihad*', identical to the Crusade in its outer, fanatical and simply religious sense. The 'greater *jihad*' is, in contrast, of the spiritual and interior order: it is the fight of man against the enemies which he bears within himself, or, more exactly, the fight of the superhuman element in man against everything which is instinctual, passionate and subject to natural forces. The condition for inner liberation is that these enemies, the 'infidels' and 'barbarians' within us, are pulled down and torn to shreds.

Now, given this background, the essence of the tradition in question lies in its conceiving the lesser war, that is, the concrete, armed one, as a path through which the 'greater *jihad*', the inner war, can be achieved, in perfect simultaneity. For this reason, in Islam, *jihad* and 'Path of God' are often synonymous. And we read in the *Qur'an*: 'So let those who sell the life of this world for the Next World fight in the Way of Allah. If someone fights in the Way of Allah, whether he is killed or is victorious, We will pay him an immense reward' (4:74).[7] And again: 'As for those who fight in the Way of Allah, He will not let their actions go astray. He will guide them and better their condition and He will admit them into the Garden which He has made known to them' (47:4-6). In these last words there is an allusion to the case of an effective death on the battlefield, which, therefore, assumes the same meaning which the expression *mors triumphalis*, triumphant

---

7   The references to the *Qur'an* and *Bhagavad-Gita* in this essay are identical to those in 'The Greater War and the Lesser War' and 'The Metaphysics of War'.

death, had in classical antiquity. But the same conception can also be taken in the symbolic sense in that the one who, while fighting the 'lesser war', has triumphed in the 'greater *jihad*' (by refusing to let himself be overcome by the current of the inferior forces aroused in his being by the vicissitudes of war, as happens in the heroism *a la* Remarque or *a la* Quinton, which we discussed in the previous article) has evoked, in any case, a force able, in principle, to overcome the crisis of death. In other words, even without having been killed one can have experienced death, can have won and can have achieved the culmination peculiar to 'supra-life'. From a higher point of view 'Paradise', 'the celestial realm', are, like Valhalla, the Greek 'Isle of Heroes', etc., only symbolic figurations, concocted for the masses, figurations which actually designate transcendent states of consciousness, beyond life and death. Ancient Aryan tradition has the word *jivanmukti*[8] to indicate a realisation of that sort obtained already in the mortal body.

Let us come now to a pure metaphysical exposition of the doctrine in question. We find it in a text originating from the ancient Indo-Aryan races, imprinted with a sense of the heroic-spiritual reality which it would be hard to match elsewhere. It is the *Bhagavad-Gita*, a part of the epic poem, the *Mahabharata*,[9] which to an expert eye contains precious material relating not only to the spirituality of the Aryan races which migrated to Asia, but to that of the 'Hyperborean' nucleus of these which, according to the traditional views to which our conception of race refers, must be considered as the origin of them all.

The *Bhagavad-Gita* contains in the shape of a dialogue the doctrine given by the incarnate divinity, Krishna, to a warrior prince, Arjuna, who had invoked him, as, overcome by humanitarian and sentimentalist scruples, he found himself no longer able to resolve to fight the enemy. The judgement of the God is categorical: it defines the mercy which had withheld Arjuna from fighting as

---

8   From the Sanskrit, this term is used in the Advaita Vedanta tradition of Vedic, or Hindu, philosophy.

9   The *Mahabharata*, along with the *Ramayana*, are the two great epic poems of the Hindu tradition. It describes the Kurukshetra War, which was an epic struggle between two branches of the royal family.

'degrading impotence' (2:4) and 'impurities...not at all befitting a man who knows the value of life. They lead not to higher planets but to infamy' (2:2). Therefore, it is not on the basis of earthly and contingent necessities but of a divine judgement that the duty of combat is confirmed here. The promise is: '[E]ither you will be killed on the battlefield and attain the heavenly planets, or you will conquer and enjoy the earthly kingdom. Therefore, get up with determination and fight' (2:37). The inner guideline, necessary to transfigure the 'lesser war' into 'greater, holy war' in death and triumphant resurrection, and to make contact, through heroic experience, with the transcendental root of one's own being, is clearly stated by Krishna: 'Therefore, O Arjuna, surrendering all your works unto Me, with full knowledge of Me, without desires for profit, with no claims to proprietorship, and free from lethargy, fight' (3:30). The terms are just as clear about the 'purity' of heroic action, which must be wanted for itself, beyond every contingent motivation, every passion and all gross utility. The words of the text are: 'Do thou fight for the sake of fighting, without consider-ing happiness or distress, loss or gain, victory or defeat – and by so doing you shall never incur sin' (2:38).

But beyond even this a true metaphysical justification of war is arrived at. We will try to express this in the most accessible way. The text works on the fundamental distinction between what in man exists in the supreme sense and, as such, is incorruptible and immutable – spirit – and the corporeal and human element, which has only an illusory existence. Having stressed the metaphysical non-reality of what one can lose or make another lose in the vicissitudes of combat, as ephemeral life and mortal body (there is nothing painful and tragic – it is said – in the fact that what is fatally destined to fall, falls), that aspect of the divine which appears as an absolute and sweeping force is recalled. Before the greatness of this force (which flashes through Arjuna's mind in the moment of a supernatural vision), every created, that is, conditioned, existence appears as a 'negation'. It can therefore be said that such a force strikes as a terrible revelation wherever such 'negation' is actively denied; that is to say, in more concrete and intelligible terms, wherever a sudden outburst sweeps up every finite life, every limitation of the petty individual, either to destroy him, or to revive him. Moreover, the secret of the 'becoming', of the fundamental restlessness and perpetual change which characterises life here below, is deduced precisely from the situation of beings, finite in themselves, which also participate in something infinite. The beings which would be described as 'created' by Christian terminology, are described rather, according to ancient Aryan tradition, as 'conditioned', subject to becoming, change and disappearance, precisely because, in them, a power burns which transcends them, which wants something infinitely vaster than all that they can ever want. Once the text in various ways has given the sense of such a vision of life it goes on to specify what fighting and heroic experience must mean for the warrior. Values change: a higher life manifests itself through death; and destruction, for the one who overcomes it, is a liberation – it is precisely in its most frightening aspects that the heroic outburst appears as a sort of manifestation of the divine in its capacity of metaphysical force of destruction of the finite – in the jargon of some modern philosophers this would be called 'the negation of the negation'. The warrior who smashes 'degarding impotence', who faces the vicissitudes of heroism 'with your mind absorbed in the supreme spirit', seizing upon a plan according to which both the 'I' and the 'thou', and therefore both fear for oneself and mercy for others, lose all meaning, can be said to assume actively the absolute divine force, to transfigure himself within it, and to free himself by breaking through the limitations relating to the mere human state of existence. 'Life – like a bow; the mind – like the arrow; the target to pierce – the supreme spirit; to join mind to spirit as the shot arrow hits its target.' – These are the evocative expressions contained in another text of the same tradition, the *Markandeya Purana*. Such, in short, is the metaphysical justification of war, the sacred interpretation of heroism, the transformation of the 'lesser war' into the 'greater holy war', according to the ancient Indo-Aryan tradition which gives us therefore, in the most complete and direct form, the intimate content present also in the other formulations pointed out.

In conclusion, let us mention two more points.

The first concerns the meaningful relation, in the *Bhagavad-Gita*, between the teaching which has just been described on the one hand and tradition and race on the other. In 4:1-3, it is said that this is the 'solar' wisdom received from Manu, who, as is well known, is the most ancient 'divine' legislator of the Aryan race. His laws, for Aryans, have the same value that the *Talmud* has for Hebrews: that is to say, they constitute the formative force of their way of life, the essence of their 'race of the spirit'. Now, this primordial wisdom, which was at first transmitted through direct succession, 'in course of time the succession was broken, and therefore the science as it is appears to be lost' (4:2). It was not to a priest, but to a warrior prince, Arjuna, that it was revealed again in the way just recounted. To realise this wisdom by following the path of sacred heroism and absolute action can only mean, therefore, restoration, awakening, resumption of what was at the origin of tradition, which has survived for centuries in the dark depths of the race and routinised itself in the customs of successive ages. The meaning that we have already indicated, the re-galvanising effect which the fact of war in given conditions can have for the 'race of the spirit', is thus exactly confirmed.

Secondly, it can be noticed that one of the main causes of the crisis of Western civilisation lies in a paralysing dilemma, constituted, on the one hand, by a weak, abstract, or conventionally devotional spirituality, rich in moralistic and humanitarian implications; and, on the other hand, by a paroxysmal development of action of all sorts, but in a materialistic and nearly barbaric sense. This situation has remote causes. Psychology teaches us that, in the subconscious, inhibition often transforms energies repressed and rejected into causes of disease and hysteria. The ancient traditions of the Aryan races were essentially characterised by the ideal of action: they were paralysed and partially suffocated by the advent of Christianity, which, in its original forms, and not without relation to elements derived from non-Aryan races, shifted the emphasis of spirituality from the domain of action to that of contemplation, devotion and monastic asceticism. Catholicism, it is true, often tried to rebuild the smashed bridge – and here, in discussing the spirit of the Crusades, we have already seen an example of this attempt. However, the antithesis between passive spirituality and un-spiritual activity has continued to weigh on the destinies of Western man and recently it has taken the form of a paroxysmal development of all sorts of action in the already stated sense of action on the material plane, which, even when it leads to realisations of unquestionable greatness, is deprived of every transcendent point of reference.

Given these conditions the advantages of the resumption of a tradition of action which is once again charged with spirit – adapted, naturally, to the times – justified not only by the immediate necessities of a particular historical situation, but by a transcendent vocation – should be clear to all. If beyond the re-integration and defence of the race of the body we must proceed to the rediscovery of values able to purify the race of the spirit of Aryan humanity from every heterogeneous element, and to lead to its steady development, we think that a new, living understanding of teachings and of ideals such as those briefly recalled here is a fitting task for us to undertake.

Soul and Race of War[1]

In the previous articles in this series we have spoken about the varieties of heroic experience and described its possible forms from the point of view of race and spirit. We here resume the argument and discuss in more detail the heroism and sense of the meaning of combat which we need to grasp as ideals in relation to our higher race and our higher tradition.

We have already been obliged to observe that, today, 'heroism' is often spoken of in a vague and unspecified sense. If by heroism what is meant is simply impulsiveness, contempt for danger, audacity and indifference towards one's own life there is in this a sort of common denominator which can put on the same level the savage, the gangster and the crusading knight. From the material point of view this generic heroism might be sufficient for many contingencies, especially in the context of mere human herds. From a higher point of view, however, we must enquire further into the question of what heroes are, and what is the meaning which leads and determines individual heroic experience.

For this problem various elements should be borne in mind, and above all those relating to the general type of civilisation, to race and, in a way, to caste as a further differentiation of race. Things can be clarified best if, as a starting point, we recall the general outline of ancient Aryan social hierarchy as it is most

---

1   Originally published on 5-20 September 1940 as 'Anima e razza della guerra' in *La Difesa della Razza*.

clearly exhibited in the Indo-Aryan civilisation, as well as in the Nordic-Romanic Medieval civilisation. This hierarchy was quadripartite. At the top were the exponents of spiritual authority – we could say, generalising, the spiritual leaders to whom the warrior nobles were subject. Then came the bourgeoisie (the 'Third Estate')[2] and, in the fourth place, the caste or class of the simple workers – today we would call them the proletariat. Evidently, this was not so much a hierarchy of men as one of functions, in which, though each function had its own dignity, the functions could not help but exist normally in the relations of subordination which have just been pointed out. It is quite clear, in fact, that these relations correspond exactly to those which exist between the various faculties of every man worthy of the name: the mind directs the will, which, in its turn, dominates the functions of the organic economy – to which, finally, the purely vital forces of the body are subordinated.

This outline is very useful, if only because it allows us to distinguish general types of civilisation, and to grasp the sense of their succession, or their alternation, in history. Thus we have four general types of civilisation, distinguished according to whether they are guided supremely by the truths, values and ideals of the spiritual leaders, the warriors, the bourgeoisie or the slaves. Leaving aside the Middle Ages, in the quadripartite hierarchy as it appeared among the Aryans of the ancient Mediterranean world, and still more among those of the Hindu-Iranian civilisation, the properly Aryan element was concentrated in the two superior castes and determined the values which dominated these cultures, while in the two other castes another blood, coming from subjugated aboriginal peoples, predominated; this fact could lead one to interesting conclusions about the racial background involved in the development of the civilisations of each of the aforementioned types.

---

2   In pre-revolutionary France, the estates were the various orders which defined the stratification of society. The Third Estate was comprised of the poorest elements of the populace.

Considerations of this nature, however, would offer little comfort to an attempt to grasp the general sense of the history of the West since it is quite clear that anyone keeping in mind the outline here explained would be led to recognise in this history, not the much-spoken-of 'evolution', but rather an 'involution' – more precisely, successive falls from each of the four hierarchical degrees to the next. It is quite clear, in fact, that civilisation of the pure heroic-sacral type can only be found in a more or less prehistoric period of the Aryan tradition. It was succeeded by civilisations at the top of which was the authority no longer of spiritual leaders, but of exponents of warrior nobility – and this is the age of the historical monarchies up to the period of revolutions. With the French and American revolutions the Third Estate becomes the most important, determining the cycle of bourgeois civilisations. Marxism and Bolshevism, finally, seem to lead to the final fall, the passage of power and authority to the hands of the last of the castes of ancient Aryan hierarchy.

Now, returning to our main argument, that is, to the typology of heroism, it should be noted that the transitions which have just been pointed out have not only a political significance, but they invest the whole sense of living and lead to the subordination of all values to those proper to the dominant caste or race of the spirit. Thus, for instance, in the first phase ethics has a supernatural justification and the supreme value is the conquest of immortality; in the second phase – that is, in the civilisation of warrior nobility – ethics is already 'secular': the ethics of fidelity, honour and loyalty. Bourgeois ethics follow this with the ideal of economic well-being, of prosperity and capitalist adventure. In the last phase the only ethics are those of materialised, collectivised and deconsecrated work as supreme value. Analogous transformations can be found in all fields – take for example architecture: as central architectonic type the temple is followed by the castle, then by the city of the commune, and finally by the rationalised hive-house of modern capitals. Another example would be the family: from a unit of the heroic-sacral type, which it was in the first phase, it passes to the type of the 'warrior' family, centred in the firm authority of the father; then follows the family as bourgeois unity on an exclusively economic-sentimental basis; and, in the last phase, there is the communist disintegration of the family.

Precisely the same articulations can be noticed in the types of heroic experience and in the meaning of war and combat in general. We do not need to dwell on the conception of war and heroism peculiar to the civilisations of the first type, or even to the original Aryans, because we have already referred repeatedly and at length to their traditions in previous articles. Here we will limit ourselves to saying that war and heroism in this first phase can be viewed essentially as forms of 'asceticism', as paths along which those same supernatural and immortality-granting fruits can be picked which are promised by initiation, or by asceticism of the religious and contemplative type. But in the second phase – in the civilisation of the 'warriors' – the perspective has already shifted; the 'sacred' content of heroic experience and the concept of war almost as symbol and glimmer of an ascending and metaphysical struggle is veiled; what is above all important now is fighting and waging war on behalf of one's race, his honour and his glory. With the advent of 'bourgeois' civilisations the type of the warrior gives way to that of the soldier and the national-territorial aspect which, only a little before, was not pronounced, but is emphasised: we are in the presence of the *citoyen*[3] who takes up arms, of the pathos of war and heroism 'for freedom', that is, more or less, for the cause of the 'immortal principle' of 'struggle against tyranny' – the jargon equivalent of the political-social forms of the previous civilisation of the warriors. It is with such 'myths' that the 1914-1918 World War has been supported, in which the Allies stated quite baldly that it represented for them the 'crusade of democracy', the new leap forward of the 'great revolution' for the cause of the freedom of the peoples against 'imperialism' and the residual forms of 'Medieval obscurantism'. In the first forms of the final phase, that is, of the 'civilisation of the slaves', the concept of war is transformed; it internationalises

---

3   French: 'citizen'.

itself and collectivises itself, tending towards the concept of the world-wide revolution of the proletariat. It is only in the service of this revolution that war is legitimate, that dying is noble and that the hero must arise from the worker. These are the fundamental meanings to which the heroic experience can conform, leaving aside its immediate and subjective aspect of impulse and boldness which lead beyond themselves.

In talking of the penultimate phase, that is, 'bourgeois war', we have deliberately spoken of 'myths'. Bourgeois nature has two main aspects: sentimentalism and economic interest. If the ideology of 'freedom', and 'nation' democratically conceived, corresponds to the first aspect, the second has no less weight in the unconfessed motives of 'bourgeois war'. The 1914-1918 war shows clearly, in fact, that the 'noble' democratic ideology was only a cover, while the part which international finance really played is now well-known. And today, in the new war, this appears even more clearly: the sentimental pretexts offered have proved to be more and more inconsistent, and it is obvious, on the contrary, that material and plutocratic interests, and the desire to maintain a monopoly upon the raw materials of the world, as well as upon gold, are what have set the 'tone' of the fight of the democratic Allies and have led them to take up arms and ask millions of men to sacrifice their lives.

This allows us also to remark upon the racial factor. We should not confuse what a caste or a class is when it is a subordinate part in a hierarchy which conforms to given values with what it becomes when it seizes power and subordinates everything to itself. Thus, the bourgeoisie and the proletariat of the modern world have characters very different from those which were characteristic of the corresponding classes in traditional Aryan civilisations. The desecrated and dark character of the former is as marked as were the sacred and spiritual superior values which, by means of participation, were reflected in the most humble and material forms of human activity of the latter. Every usurpation has a degradation as its fatal consequence: this process almost always presupposes the infiltration of socially and racially inferior

elements. In the case of the Western bourgeoisie these elements
have been supplied by Hebraism. Let us not delude ourselves: the
type of the plutocrats and of the capitalists, the three kings of
bourgeois and democratic civilisation, is essentially a Jewish type,
even when precise physical descent from the Jewish race cannot
be demonstrated. With respect to America, everyone knows the
considerations which led Sombart[4] to call capitalism the quintes-
sence of the doctrine of Moses. It is well-known that, in the final
phase of the normal society of the West which was the Ghibelline Middle Ages, international trade and commerce using gold
were to a large extent Jewish prerogatives, and that, even in the
'bourgeois professions' of the Third Estate of that time, wherever
they remained in the hands of Aryans, before the emancipation
and degeneration of the civilisation of the Communes, features
of great dignity and probity were maintained which can hardly be
found in the modern civilisation of the merchants, i.e., the bourgeois capitalist civilisation. It is essentially from the Jewish element
that this civilisation has drawn its 'style'. And, given these facts, it
is obvious that, by means of elective affinities, this civilisation had
to be completely opened to Hebraism, which has scaled its main
positions of responsibility with ease, and has taken over control
of all its powers by means of its own specialised racial qualities.

   Thus, it can well be said that the current war is one of merchants and Jews, who have mobilised the armed forces and the
heroic possibilities of democratic nations to defend their interests.
Certainly, there are other contributory factors. But it is unquestionable that England is a typical case of this phenomenon,
which is hardly new, and, to tell the truth, exhibits a characteristic
phenomenon of inversion. To be specific, in England monarchy
and nobility still exist and, until yesterday, a military class with an
unquestionable heritage of character, sang-froid and contempt for
danger existed also. But it is not in such elements that the centre
of the British Empire lies, but rather in the Jew and the Judaised
Aryan. The degenerate remains of a 'civilisation of warriors' serve

---

4   Werner Sombart (1863-1941), a German economist, and the author of *The Jews
     and Modern Capitalism* (London: T. F. Unwin, 1913).

a 'civilisation of merchants', which – normally – would rather have had to serve them. Only those who have a precise sense of this can grasp the dark and confused forces at work in the race of those whom Italy fights today: and it is precisely the character of these forces which explains the decline of English fighting ability, and the impossibility of true heroism and true boldness because by now even the 'mythic' premises of the 1914-1918 war are lacking, as has been pointed out just above.

Let us come now to our final point, which is the clarification of the sense of our war and our heroism on the basis of the general doctrinal and historical views we have expressed. At the risk of being taken for hopeless Utopians we will never grow tired of repeating that our taking up once more of the Aryan and Roman symbols must lead to the taking up once more, also, of the spiritual and traditional conceptions which were peculiar to the original civilisations which developed under those symbols.

We have spoken of the superior Aryan conception of war and heroism as asceticism, catharsis, overcoming of the tie of the human 'I' and, ultimately, effective participation in immortality. Now let us emphasise that the inferior is comprised in the superior – meaning, in our case, that the experience of combat according to this superior meaning must not be understood as a sort of confused mystical impulsiveness, but as the development, integration and transfiguration of everything which can be experienced in war, or which can be asked of war, from any of the subordinate and conditioned standpoints. Proceeding from what is below to what is above, it can therefore be said that an unavoidable need for social justice in the international arena and a revolt against the hegemony of nations incarnating the 'civilisation of the merchants' may be the immediate determinant of the war. But the one who fights the war on such grounds can find in it also the occasion to realise, simultaneously, a higher experience, that is, fighting and being a hero not so much as soldier but as warrior, as a man who fights and loves to fight not so much in the interest of material conquests as in the name of his King and of his tradition. And beyond this stage, in a successive phase, or a higher class, this same war can become a means to achieve war in the supreme sense, as asceticism and 'path of God', as culmination of that general meaning of living, of which it was said: *vita est militia super terram*. All this becomes integrated and – it can be added – there is no doubt that the impulse and the ability to sacrifice are superior by far in the one who realises this supreme meaning in war, as compared one who stops at one of the subordinate meanings. And even on this mundane plane the law of the earth can meet with the law of God when the most tragic demands which can be made in the name of the greatness of a nation are fulfilled in an action whose ultimate sense is, however, the overcoming of the human tie, contempt for the petty existence of the 'plains', the tension which, in the supreme culminations of life, means choosing something which is more than life.

If this is the idea of the 'holy war' as simultaneously material and spiritual struggle which was peculiar to the Aryan peoples, a further, specific reference to Aryan Romanity is opportune to avoid some 'romantic' distortions to which that idea has been subjected in a later period in some stocks of that people, above all Nordic ones. We mean to allude to so-called 'tragic heroism', the love of combat for its own sake, which among Nordic peoples takes on overtones of the Titanic, the 'Nibelungian'[5] and the Faustian. To the extent that this is not just literature – and bad literature – it contains glints of Aryan spirituality, certainly, but they have degenerated to the level appropriate to a simple civilisation of warriors since they have not been able to remain on the superior level of the origins, which is not merely heroic, but also 'solar' and 'Olympian'. The Roman conception does not know this distortion. Inwardly, as outwardly, war cannot be the last word; it is rather the means to conquest of a power as calm as it is perfect and intangible. Beyond the mysticism of war, in the higher Aryan conception as well as in the Roman one, is the mysticism

---

5   Nibelungen is the name of the Burgundian royal family in Germanic mythology.

of victory. The soldiers of Fabius[6] did not romantically swear to win or to die, but rather to return as victors – as they indeed did. In the Roman ceremony of the triumph, which, as we said in another article, had a more religious than military character, the personality of the victor was in the closest relation with Jupiter, the Aryan god of cosmic order and law. The authentic idea of *Pax Romana*[7] had distinctly 'Olympian' characteristics – to realise this all one needs to do is to refer to the writers of the age of Augustus[8] and to Virgil[9] above all. It is not the cessation of the spiritual tension of war, but its fecund and luminous culmination – as such, it represents the overcoming of war as an end-in-itself and obscurely tragic vocation.

These are the fundamental characteristic elements of the highest Aryan conception of combat. The importance of recalling them and experiencing them again today cannot be doubted by anyone who is aware that the current conflict is not merely an almost 'private' affair between certain nations, but is destined, by destroying confused and violently established situations, to lead to a new general order, truly worthy of the name: spiritually Roman.

6   Quintus Fabius Maximus Verrucosus (280 BC?-203 BC) was a Roman consul who was appointed dictator of the Roman Republic after its initial defeat during the Second Punic War, in which Rome was invaded by the Carthaginians under Hannibal's command. Fabius managed to keep the stronger Carthaginian force at bay by engaging in a protracted guerilla war against them, rather than by confronting them directly, which he knew would lead to defeat. For his victorious service, the Romans hailed Fabius as 'The Shield of Rome'.

7   'The Roman Peace', this was a period of the history of the Roman Empire, lasting roughly from 27 BC to 180 AD, during which the Empire prospered and fought no major wars.

8   Augustus (63 BC-14 AD) was the first Emperor of the Roman Empire who initiated the *Pax Romana*.

9   Virgil (70-19 BC) was a Roman poet who authored the *Aeneid*, which was the national epic of Classical Rome.

The Aryan Doctrine of Combat and Victory[1]

The decline of the modern West, according to the view of a famous critic of civilisation,[2] clearly possesses two salient characteristics: in the first place the pathological development of activity for its own sake; in the second place contempt for the values of knowledge and contemplation.

By knowledge this critic does not mean rationalism, intellectualism or the vain games of men of letters – nor by contemplation does he mean cutting oneself off from the world, renunciation or a misunderstood form of monastic detachment. Knowledge and contemplation represent for him, rather, the most normal and appropriate forms of participation of man in supernatural, superhuman and supra-rational reality. Notwithstanding this clarification, his view involves what is, to us, an unacceptable presupposition. In fact, he has already tacitly implied that every act in the material domain is limiting and that the highest spiritual sphere is accessible only in ways different from those of action.

---

1   Originally published as *Die arische Lehre von Kampf und Sieg* (Vienna: Anton Schroll & Co., 1941), comprising the text of the address given by Evola in German at the Abteilung für Kulturwissenschaft des Kaisers Wilhelm-Instituts conference, at the Palazzo Zuccari in Rome on 7 December 1940.

2   The critic referred to is probably René Guénon.

In this premise the influence of a vision of life is clearly recognisable which, in its essence, remains strange to the spirit of the Aryan race, even if it is so embedded in the thought of the Christianised West that it can even be found revived in the imperial conception of Dante.[3] The opposition between action and contemplation, however, was unknown to the ancient Aryans. Action and contemplation were not regarded as the two terms of an opposition. They designated merely two distinct paths to the same spiritual realisation. In other words, it was thought that man could overcome the conditioning of individuality and participate in the supernatural reality by means of contemplation or, equally, by means of action.

Starting from this conception we must therefore evaluate the character of the decline of Western civilisation in a different way. The tradition of action is in the nature of the Aryan-Western races. This tradition has, however, undergone a progressive deviation. The modern West has thus come to know and honour only a secularised and materialised form of action, devoid of any point of contact with transcendence – a desecrated activity, which has necessarily degenerated fatally into fever and mania and become action for the sake of action, merely producing simple mechanical effects conditioned by time. In the modern world ascetic and authentically contemplative values cannot be drawn into correspondence with such degenerate action either, but only a confused culture and a lifeless and conventional faith. This is the point of reference for our analysis of the situation.

If the watchword for any current movement of renewal is 'return to the origins' then recovering awareness of the ancient Aryan conception of action must be considered an essential task. This conception must operate with transformative effectiveness, evoking vital forces in the new man, aware of his race. Today, we ourselves propose to attempt a general survey of the speculative universe of the ancient Aryans in order to provide new evidence

---

3   Dante Alighieri (1265-1321) is regarded as the greatest writer in the Italian language and was the author of *The Divine Comedy*. Here, Evola is likely referring to Dante's work of political philosophy, *Monarchy* (Cambridge: Cambridge University Press, 1996).

for some fundamental elements of our common tradition, with particular relevance to the meaning of combat, war and victory.

* * *

For the ancient Aryan war had the general meaning of a perpetual fight between metaphysical powers. On the one hand there was the Olympian principle of light, the uranic and solar reality; on the other hand, brute violence, the titanic-telluric, barbaric element in the classical sense, the feminine-demonic substance. The motif of this metaphysical fight resurfaces continually through countless forms of myth in all traditions of Aryan origin. Any fight, in the material sense, was experienced with greater or lesser awareness as an episode in that antithesis. But the Aryan race considered itself to be the army of the Olympian principle: accordingly, it is necessary to restore this conception among Aryans, as being the justification, or the highest consecration, of any hegemonic aspiration, but also of the very idea of empire, whose anti-secular character is basically very obvious.

To the traditionally based world view, all apparent realities are symbolic. This is therefore true of war as well, as is seen from the subjective and interior point of view. War and the Path of God are thus merged into a single entity.

The significant testimonies found within the Nordic-German traditions regarding this are well-known. It is necessary to note, however, that these traditions, in the terms in which they have reached us, have become fragmented and jumbled up, or constitute materialistic residues of higher, primordial Aryan traditions, often decayed to the level of popular superstitions. This consideration does not prevent us from establishing some essential motifs.

First of all, as is well-known, Valhalla is the centre of celestial immortality, reserved mainly for heroes fallen on the battlefield. The lord of this place, Odin-Wotan, is presented to us in the *Ynglingasaga* as having shown to the heroes the path which leads to the place of the gods, where immortal life flourishes. According to this tradition no sacrifice or cult is more appreciated by the supreme god, and none produces richer fruits, than that sacrifice which one offers as one falls fighting on the battlefield. In addition to this, behind the confused popular representation of the *Wildes Heer*[4] this meaning is hidden: through the warriors who, falling, offer a sacrifice to Odin the power is increased which this god needs for the ultimate battle against the *Ragna-rökkr*, that is, the 'darkening of the divine', which has threatened the world since ancient times. This illustrates clearly the Aryan motif of the metaphysical struggle. In the *Edda*, it is said that 'no matter how great the number of the heroes gathered in Valhalla they will never be too many for when the Wolf comes'. The 'Wolf' here is the symbol of dark and wild powers which the world of the Aesir had managed to chain and subdue.

The Aryo-Iranian conception of Mithra, the 'sleepless warrior', who at the head of the Fravashi of his faithful wages battle against the enemies of the Aryan God of Light is completely analogous. We will soon deal with the Fravashi and their correspondence with the Valkyries of the Nordic tradition. For now, we would like to explain the general meaning of the 'holy war' by means of other, concordant testimonies.

It should not cause surprise if we refer in the first place to the Muslim tradition. Here, the Muslim tradition serves as transmitter of the Aryo-Iranian tradition. The idea of 'holy war' – at least as far as the elements that we are considering are concerned – reached the Arabian tribes via the world of Persian speculation. It was, therefore, a late rebirth of a primordial Aryan heritage, and seen from this perspective we can certainly adopt it.

Having said that, in the tradition in question two 'holy wars' are distinguished: the 'greater holy war' and the 'lesser holy war'. The distinction is based on a saying of the Prophet, who, when

---

4   German: 'wild host'. This is a concept present in many ancient cultures in which a group of hunters on horseback can be seen pursuing their prey across the sky. In some versions the hunters are believed to be the souls of dead warriors being led by the gods.

he got back from a military expedition, said, 'I return now from the lesser to the greater war'.[5]

In this respect the greater holy war belongs to the spiritual order. The lesser holy war, in contrast, is the physical struggle, the material war, fought in the outer world. The greater holy war is the struggle of man against the enemies he bears in himself. More precisely, it is the fight of the supernatural element, innate in man, against everything which is instinctual, passionate, chaotic and subject to the forces of nature. This is also the idea that reveals itself in a text of the ancient Aryan warrior wisdom, the *Bhagavad-Gita*: 'Thus knowing oneself to be transcendental to the material senses, mind and intelligence, O mighty-armed Arjuna, one should steady the mind by deliberate spiritual intelligence and thus – by spiritual strength – conquer this insatiable enemy known as lust' (3:43).

The necessary condition for the inner work of liberation is that this enemy is destroyed once and for all. In the context of a heroic tradition the lesser holy war – that is, external combat – serves only as something by means of which the greater holy war is achieved. For this reason 'holy war' and 'Path of God' are often treated as synonymous in the texts. Thus we read in the *Qur'an*: 'So let those who sell the life of this world for the Next World fight in the Way of Allah. If someone fights in the Way of Allah, whether he is killed or is victorious, We will pay him an immense reward' (4:74). And further: 'As for those who fight in the Way of Allah, He will not let their actions go astray. He will guide them and better their condition and He will admit them into the Garden which He has made known to them' (47:4-6).

This is an allusion to physical death in war, which corresponds perfectly to the so-called *mors triumphalis* – 'triumphant death' – of the Classical traditions. However, the same doctrine can also be interpreted in a symbolic sense. The one who, in the 'lesser holy war', has been able to live a 'greater holy war' has created within himself a force which puts him in a position to overcome the

---

5   All references to Islamic scriptures and the *Bhagavad-Gita* in this essay are identical to those contained in 'The Greater War and the Lesser War' and 'Metaphysics of War'.

crisis of death. Even without getting killed physically, through the asceticism of action and combat, one can experience death, one can win inwardly and realise 'more-than-life'. In the esoteric respect, as a matter of fact, 'paradise', 'the celestial realm' and analogous expressions are nothing but symbolic representations – concocted for the people – of transcendent states of conscious- ness on a higher plane than life and death.

These considerations should allow us to discern the same contents and meanings, under the outer garment of Christianity, which the Nordic-Western heroic tradition was forced to wear during the Crusades in order to be able to manifest itself in the external world. In the ideology of the Crusade the liberation of the Temple and the conquest of the 'Holy Land' had points of contact – much more numerous than one is generally inclined to believe – with the Nordic-Aryan tradition, which refers to the mystical Asgard, the remote land of the Aesir and heroes, where death does not reign and the inhabitants enjoy immortal life and supernatural peace. Holy war appeared as an integrally spiritual war, so much so that it could be compared literally by preachers to 'a bathing which is almost like the fire of purgatory, but before death'.

Saint Bernard declared to the Templars, 'It is a glory for you never to leave the battle [unless] covered with laurels. But it is an even greater glory to earn on the battlefield an immortal crown ...'

The 'absolute glory' – attributed to the Lord who is above, in the skies – *in excelsis Deo*[6] – is ordained also for the Crusader. Against this background Jerusalem, the coveted goal of the 'lesser holy war', could be seen in the twofold aspect of terrestrial city and celestial city and the Crusade proved to be the prelude to a true fulfilment of immortality.

The oscillating military vicissitudes of the Crusades provoked bafflement, initial confusion and even a wavering of faith. But later their sole effect was to purify the idea of holy war from every residue of materiality. The ill-fated outcome of a Crusade came to be compared to virtue persecuted by misfortune, a virtue

---

6 Latin: 'God in the highest'.

whose value can be judged and rewarded only in the light of a supra-terrestrial life. Beyond victory or defeat the judgement of value focused on the spiritual dimension of action. Thus, the holy war was worthwhile for its own sake, irrespective of its visible results, as a means to reach a supra-personal realisation through the active sacrifice of the human element.

The same teaching appears, elevated to a metaphysical plane of expression, in a famous Hindu-Aryan text – the *Bhagavad-Gita*. The humanitarian compassion and the emotions which hold the warrior Arjuna back from fighting against the enemy are characterised by the god as 'impurities…not at all befitting a man who knows the value of life. They lead not to higher planets but to infamy' (2:2).

Instead the god promises the following: '[E]ither you will be killed on the battlefield and attain the heavenly planets, or you will conquer and enjoy the earthly kingdom. Therefore, get up with determination and fight' (2:37).

The inner disposition to transmute the lesser holy war into the greater holy war is clearly described in the following terms: 'Thus knowing oneself to be transcendental to the material senses, mind and intelligence, O mighty-armed Arjuna, one should steady the mind by deliberate spiritual intelligence and thus – by spiritual strength – conquer this insatiable enemy known as lust' (3:43).

Equally clear expressions assert the purity of this action: it must be wanted for itself, beyond every material aim, beyond every passion and every human impulse: 'Do thou fight for the sake of fighting, without considering happiness or distress, loss or gain, victory or defeat – and by so doing you shall never incur sin' (2:38).

As a further metaphysical foundation the god enlightens his listener on the difference between absolute spirit, which is indestructible, and the corporeal and human elements, which possess only illusory existence. On the one hand Arjuna becomes aware of the metaphysical unreality of what one can lose or cause others to lose, i.e., the ephemeral life and the mortal body. On the other hand Arjuna is led to experience the manifestation of the divine as a power which sweeps the one who experiences it away into irresistible absoluteness. Compared to this force any conditioned form of existence appears as a mere negation. When this negation is itself continuously and actively negated, that is, when every limited form of existence is overwhelmed or destroyed in combat, this force becomes terrifyingly evident. It is in these terms that the energy suitable to provoke the heroic transformation of the individual can be properly defined. To the extent that he is able to act in the purity and absoluteness which we have indicated the warrior breaks the chains of the human, evokes the divine as metaphysical force of destruction of the finite, and attracts this force effectively into himself, finding in it his illumination and liberation. The evocative watchword of another text, belonging to the same tradition, is appropriate here: 'Life – like a bow; the mind – like the arrow; the target to pierce – the supreme spirit; to join mind to spirit as the shot arrow hits its target.'

It is highly significant that the *Bhagavad-Gita* presents these teachings, which explain how the higher form of the metaphysical realisation of combat and heroism should be understood as referring to a primordial Aryan heritage of a solar nature. These teachings were in fact given by 'The Sun' to the primordial legislator of the Aryans, Manu, and subsequently maintained by a sacred dynasty of kings. In the course of centuries they came to be lost and were therefore newly revealed by the divinity, not to a priest, but to a representative of the warrior nobility, Arjuna.

* * *

What we have discussed so far allows us to understand also the intimate content of another group of classical and Nordic traditions. We must start with a simple observation: in these traditions, certain specific symbolic images appear exceptionally often: that of the soul as demon, double, genius and the like; those of the Dionysian[7] entities and the goddess of death; and,

---

7   Dionysus was the Greek god of ecstasy and intoxication.

finally, that of a goddess of victory, who often appears also as goddess of battle.

To understand these we should first clarify the meaning of the image of the soul as demon, genius or double. The man of Classical Antiquity symbolised in the demon or double a deep force, which is the life of life, so to speak, insofar as it rules over all the corporeal and animic events which ordinary consciousness does not reach, but which, however, are determinative of the contingent existence and destiny of the individual. A close relationship was believed to exist between this entity and the mystical powers of race and blood. The demon seems in many aspects to be similar to the *lares*, the mystical entities of a stock or of a progeny, of which Macrobius,[8] for example, asserts: 'The gods are those who keep us alive – they feed our body and guide our soul.' It can be said that there is a relationship between the demon and ordinary consciousness analogous to that which exists between the individuating principle and the individuated principle. The former is, according to the teaching of the ancients, a supra-individual force, superior, therefore, to birth and death. The latter, i.e., individuated consciousness, conditioned by the body and the outer world, is destined as a rule to dissolution or to an ephemeral and indistinct survival. In the Nordic tradition, the image of the Valkyrie has more or less the same meaning as that of the demon in Classical Antiquity. In many texts the image of the Valkyrie merges with that of the *fylgja*, that is, a spiritual entity at work in man, to whose power the destiny of man is subject. And as *kynfylgja* the Valkyrie is – like the *lares* of ancient Rome – the mystical power of the blood. The same thing applies to the Fravashi of the Aryo-Iranian tradition. The Fravashi, a famous Orientalist explains, 'is the intimate power of any human being, it is what keeps him alive and sees to it that he is born and exists'.

At the same time the Fravashi are, like Roman *lares*, related to the primordial powers of a stock, and are, like the Valkyries, terrifying goddesses of war, dispensers of fortune and victory.

---

8   Ambrosius Theodosius Macrobius (395-423), a Roman Neoplatonist philosopher. His primary work is the *Saturnalia* (New York: Columbia University Press, 1969).

This is the first connection we wish to examine. This mysterious power, which is the deep soul of the race and the transcendent factor at work in the individual, what can it have in common with the goddess of war? To understand this point correctly, it is necessary to remember that ancient Indo-Europeans had, so to speak, an aristocratic and differentiated conception of immortality. Not all escape the dissolution of the 'I' into that lemuric residuum of which Hades and Niflheim[9] were ancient symbolic representations. Immortality is the privilege of the few, and, according to the Aryan conception, specifically the privilege of heroes. Continuing to live – not as a shadow, but as a demigod – is reserved to those which a special spiritual action has elevated from the one nature to the other. Here, we unfortunately cannot prove *in extenso* the following affirmation: from the operative standpoint this spiritual action consisted of the transformation of the individual 'I' from the form of ordinary human consciousness, which remains circumscribed and individuated, into a deep, supra-individual and individuating power, which exists beyond birth and death, a power to which we have said the notion of the 'demon' corresponds.[10]

The demon is, however, beyond all the finite forms in which it manifests itself, and this not only because it represents the primordial power of an entire stock, but also with respect to intensity. Consequently, the abrupt passage from ordinary consciousness to the power symbolised by the demon causes a destructive crisis, a sort of rupture, as a result of the tension of a potential too strong for the human circuit. Let us suppose therefore the case in which, in completely exceptional conditions, the demon can itself, so to speak, burst out in the individual, making him feel its destroying transcendence: in this case a sort of living and active experience of death would be aroused. The second connection, that is, the reason why in the mythical representations of Antiquity the image of the double or demon has been able to merge

---

9 In Norse mythology Niflheim was the location of Hel, which is where the souls of those who die unheroic deaths were sent.

10 For a more precise understanding of the general conception of life in which the teachings mentioned here are based, we refer the reader to our *Revolt*. (Note added by Evola).

with that of the divinity of death, therefore becomes clear. In the Nordic tradition the warrior sees his Valkyrie as he dies or he experiences a mortal danger.

Let us go further. In religious asceticism mortification, the renunciation of the 'I' and the impulse to give oneself up to God, are the preferred means by which one attempts to cause the aforementioned crisis and to overcome it effectively. Expressions like 'mystical death' or 'dark night of the soul',[11] etc., which indicate this condition, are well-known. As opposed to this, in the context of a heroic tradition the active impulse, the Dionysian unleashing of the element of action, is the preferred means to the same end. At the lowest degree of the corresponding phenomenology we observe, for example, dance when employed as a sacred technique to evoke and employ, through the ecstasy of the soul, forces which reside in its depths. Another life arises within the life of the individual when freed by the Dionysian rhythm, almost like the emergence of his own abysmal root. The Wildes Heer, the Furies,[12] the Erynnyes and other analogous spiritual natures are symbolic representations of this force. They therefore correspond to a manifestation of the demon in its terrifying and active transcendence. Sacred games represent a higher level of this process. A still higher level is that of war. In this way we are led back again to the ancient Aryan conception of combat and warrior asceticism.

The possibility of some such supra-normal experience was acknowledged to reside at the peak of danger and of heroic combat. The Latin word *ludere* (to play, to fight) already seems to contain the idea of resolving (Bruckmann)[13]. This is one of the many references to the property, innate to combat, of freeing one from individual limitation and of bringing to emergence free forces which are latent in the depths. The third analogy draws its

---

11 This is the title of a work by St. John of the Cross.

12 In Roman mythology, the Furies were female deities who took revenge on the living on behalf of dead people who had been wronged. Their name in Greek mythology was the Erynnyes.

13 Heinz Bruckmann, a German scholar of Latin.

origin and foundation from this: the demon, the *lares*, the individuating 'I', etc., are identical not only to the Furies, the Erynnyes, and other unleashed Dionysian natures, which themselves have numerous features in common with the goddess of death; they correspond also to the virgins who guide the attacker in battle, the Valkyries and the Fravashi. The Fravashi, for example, are referred to in the texts as "the terrifying, the omnipotent", "those who storm and grant victory to the one who invokes them" – or, to say it better, to the one who evokes them within himself.

It is a short step from here to our final analogy. The same warlike entities assume finally in Aryan traditions the features of goddesses of victory, a metamorphosis which marks precisely the happy fulfilment of the inner experiences in question. Just like the demon or double they signify a deep and supra-individual power, which remains in its latent state during ordinary consciousness; just as the Furies and the Erynnyes reflect a special manifestation of demonic eruptions and outbursts – and the goddesses of death, Valkyries, *fravashi*, etc. refer to the same situations, insofar as these are made possible by means of heroic combat – so the goddess of victory is the expression of the triumph of the 'I' over this power. It marks the successful impulsion towards a condition situated beyond the danger innate in the ecstasy and the sub-personal forms of destruction, a danger always waiting in ambush behind the frenetic moment of Dionysian action and of heroic action itself. What finds expression in this representation of mythical consciousness is therefore the impulse towards a spiritual, truly supra-personal state, which makes free, immortal, inwardly indestructible – which, as it is said, "makes, of the two, one" (the two elements of the human essence).

Let us come now to the overall meaning of these ancient heroic traditions, that is, to the mystical conception of victory. The fundamental idea was that there was an effective correspondence between the physical and the metaphysical, between the visible and the invisible; a correspondence whereby the works of the spirit manifested supra-individual features and were expressed through real operations and facts. From this presupposition, a spiritual realisation was pre-ordained as the secret spirit of certain warlike enterprises of which concrete victory would be the crown. Accordingly, the material, military dimension of victory was regarded as the correlative of a spiritual fact, which brought the victory about in accordance with the necessary relationship between the interior and exterior worlds. Victory, then, appears as the outward and visible sign of a consecration and a mystical rebirth achieved at the same point. The Furies and death, whom the warrior has faced materially on the battlefield, contested spiritually within him in the form of a threatening eruption of the primordial forces of his being. As he triumphs over these, victory is his.

It thus becomes clear why, in the traditional world, victory assumed a sacred meaning. Thus, the chieftain, acclaimed on the battlefield, provided a living experience of the presence of a mystical power which transfigured him. The deep meaning of the other-worldly character bursting out in the glory and the 'divinity' of the victor – the fact that, in ancient Rome, the celebration of the triumph assumed features much more sacred than military – becomes therefore comprehensible. The recurrent symbolism in ancient Aryan traditions of victories, Valkyries and analogous entities which guide the soul of the warrior to the 'sky', is revealed to us in a completely different light now, as does the myth of the victorious hero, such as the Dorian Hercules, who obtains the crown which makes him share in Olympian immortality from Nike, the 'goddess of victory'. The extent to which the perspective which wants to see only 'poetry', rhetoric and fables in all this is distorted and superficial becomes clear now.

Mystical theology teaches that the beatifying spiritual vision is achieved in glory, and Christian iconography puts the aureole of glory around the heads of saints and of martyrs. All this indicates a heritage, albeit faded, of our more elevated heroic tradition. The Aryo-Iranian tradition already knew, in fact, glory – *hvareno* – understood as celestial fire, a glory which comes down on kings and chiefs, renders them immortal and in victory testifies for them. And, in classical Antiquity, the radiating royal crown symbolised glory precisely as solar and celestial fire. In the Aryan world light, solar splendour, glory, victory, divine royalty are images and notions which appear in the tightest conjunction, not in the sense of abstractions and inventions of man, but rather with the meaning of latent potentialities and absolutely real actualised capacities. In such context the mystical doctrine of fight and victory represents for us a luminous apex of our common tradition of action.

* * *

Today this tradition speaks to us in a way which is still comprehensible – provided, of course, that we renounce its outer and contingent modalities of manifestation. If we want to go beyond an exhausted, battered spirituality, built upon speculative abstractions and pietistic feelings, and at the same time to go beyond the materialistic degeneration of action, what better points of reference can be found today than the aforementioned ideals of ancient Aryan man?

But there is more. In the West spiritual and material tensions have become entangled to such a degree in recent years that they can only be resolved through combat. With the present war an age goes towards its end and forces are gaining ground which can no longer be dominated by abstract ideas, universalistic principles or myths conceived as mere irrationalities, and which do not in themselves provide the basis for a new civilisation. A far deeper and far more essential form of action is now necessary so that, beyond the ruins of a subverted and condemned world, a new age breaks through for Europe.

In this perspective a lot will depend on the way in which the individual of today is able to give shape to the living experience of combat: that is, on whether he is in a position to assume heroism and sacrifice as catharsis, and as a means of liberation and of inner awakening. This work of our combatants – inner, invisible, far from gestures and grandiloquences – will have a decisive character not only for the conclusion, victorious and definitive, of the events of this stormy period, but also for the configuration and the attribution of the sense of the Order which will rise from victory. Combat is necessary to awaken and temper that force which, beyond onslaughts, blood and danger, will favour a new creation with a new splendour and a powerful peace.

For this reason it is on the battlefield that pure action must be learned again today: action not only in the sense of virile asceticism, but also in the sense of purification and of path towards higher forms of life, forms valid in themselves and for themselves – this means precisely a return to ancient Aryo-Western tradition. From remote times, this evocative watchword still echoes down to us: 'Life – like a bow; the mind – like the arrow; the target to pierce – the supreme spirit; to join mind to spirit as the shot arrow hits its target.'

The one who still experiences combat today, in the sense of this acknowledgement of this profession, will remain standing while others will collapse – and his will be an invincible force. This new man will overcome within himself any drama, any dusk, any chaos, forming, with the advent of the new times, the principle of a new development. According to the ancient Aryan tradition such heroism of the best men can assume a real evocative function, that is, it can re-establish the contact, lost for centuries, between world and supra-world. Then the meaning of combat will be, not horrible slaughter, nor desolate destiny conditioned by the will-to-power alone, but a test of the good reason and divine vocation of a stock. Then the meaning of peace will not be renewed drowning in colourless bourgeois everyday life, nor the lack of the spiritual tension found in combat, but the fullness of the tension itself.

'The blood of Heroes is closer to the Lord than the ink of scholars and the prayers of the pious.'

The traditional conception is also based on the presupposition that, far more than individuals, the mystical primordial powers of the race are at work in 'holy war'. These powers of the origins are those which create world-wide empires and bring to men 'victorious peace'.

The Meaning of the Warrior
Element for the New Europe[1]

One of the main oppositions which the First World War brought to light concerns the relationship between the state and the military element. What appeared was a characteristic antithesis, which in reality reflected not so much two different groups of people as two different ages, two mentalities and two different conceptions of 'civilisation'.

On one hand one found the idea that the military and, more generally, the warrior element is merely subordinate and instrumental to the state. The normal and correct rulers of the state, according to this view, are what one might call the 'civil' or 'bourgeois' element. This 'bourgeois' element engages in professional politics and – to use a well-known expression – when politics must be continued by other means,[2] the military forces are employed. Under these conditions the military element is not expected to exercise any particular influence on politics or on the life in society in general. It is acknowledged, certainly, that the military element

---

1 Originally published in March 1941 as 'Sul significato dell'elemento guerriero per la nuova Europa' in *La Vita Italiana*.

2 'We see, therefore, that War is not merely a political act, but also a real political instrument, a continuation of political commerce, a carrying out of the same by other means.' A famous quotation from Claus von Clausewitz (1780-1831), a Prussian military theorist. The quotation can be found in his book *On War* (London: Routledge, 2004), p. 42.

has its own ethics and values. However, this view considers it undesirable, and even absurd, to apply these ethics and values to the entire normal life of the nation. The view in question is in fact closely related to the democratic, *illuminé*[3] and liberal belief that true civilisation does not have anything to do with that sad necessity which is war, but that its foundation, rather than the warlike virtues, is 'the progress of the arts and sciences' and the formation of social life according to the 'immortal principles'. That is why, in such a society, one should speak of a 'soldier' element rather than a true warrior element. In fact, etymologically the word 'soldier' refers to troops which fight for a salary or a fee in the service of a class which does not itself wage war. This is, more or less, the meaning which, in spite of obligatory conscription, the military element has in liberal and democratic-bourgeois States. These States use it to resolve serious disputes on the international plane more or less in the same way as, in the domestic order, they use the police.

Over and against this view there is the other according to which the military element permeates the political, and also the ethical, order. Military values here are authentic warrior values and have a fundamental part in the general ideal of an ethical formation of life; an ideal valid also, therefore, beyond the strictly military plane and periods of war. The result is a limitation of the civilian bourgeoisie, politically, and of the bourgeois spirit in general in all sectors of social life. True civilisation is conceived of here in virile, active and heroic terms: and it is on this basis that the elements which define all human greatness, and the real rights of the peoples, are understood.

It hardly needs to be said that, in the 1914-1918 World War, the former ideology was proper to the Allies and above all to the western and Atlantic democracies, while the latter was essentially represented by the Central Powers. According to a well-known Masonic watchword – which we have often recalled here – that war

---

3   French: 'enlightened'.

was fought as a sort of great crusade of worldwide democracy[4] against 'militarism' and 'Prussianism', which, to those 'imperialist' nations, represented 'obscurantist' residues within 'developed' Europe.

This expression contains, however, the truth which we pointed out at the beginning, namely that the opposition was not only between two groups of peoples but also between two ages – even though, naturally, at the time and subjectively things appeared in a very different manner. What were called in the Masonic jargon 'anachronistic residues' meant really the survival of values peculiar to the whole of traditional, warlike, virile and Aryan Europe, while the values of the 'developed world' did not mean anything but the ethical and spiritual decline of the West. Moreover, we know better now what 'imperialists' the hypocritical exponents of this latter world were in their own peculiar way: theirs was, to be exact, the imperialism of the bourgeoisie and the merchants who wanted to enjoy undisturbed the benefits of peace, which was to be imposed and preserved, not so much by their own military forces as by forces enlisted from all parts of the world and paid for this purpose.

With the peace treaties and the developments of the post-war period this has become more and more evident. The function of the military element deteriorated into that of a sort of international police force – or, rather than really 'international', a police force organised by a certain group of nations to impose, against the will of the others and for their own profit, a given actual situation: since this was, and is, what 'the defence of peace' and 'the rights of nations' really mean. The decline of all feelings of warrior-like pride and honour was subsequently demonstrated by the fact that all sorts of ignoble means were developed to secure the desired results without even having to resort to this army degraded to the status of international police: systems of sanctions, economic blockades, national boycotts, etc.

---

4   When the United States entered the war in 1917, President Woodrow Wilson characterised it as a 'crusade for democracy'.

With the most recent international developments which have led to the loss of authority of the League of Nations and, finally, to the current war, an effective reversal of values, not only on the political plane but also on the ethical one and in general of life-view as a whole, has become clearly visible. The current battle is not so much against a particular people but rather against a particular idea, which is more or less the same as the one supported by the Allies in the previous war. That war was intended to consolidate 'democratic imperialism' against any dangerous troublemakers; the new war is intended to mark the end of this 'imperialism' and of several myths which serve it as 'alibis', and to create the preconditions for a new age in which warrior ethics are to serve as the basis for the civilisation of the collective of European peoples. In this sense the present war can be called a restorative war. It restores to their original standing the ideals and the views of life and right which are central to the original traditions of the Aryan peoples – above all the Aryo-Roman and Nordic-Aryan ones – so central that, when they decayed or were abandoned, this led inevitably to the fall of each of those peoples and power passed into the hands of inferior elements, both racially and spiritually.

It is, however, advisable that misunderstandings do not arise about the meaning which the warrior element will have in the new Europe, focusing on the word 'militarism', similar to those already deliberately fostered – with full knowledge of the facts – by the democratic adversaries. It is not a matter of confining Europe to barracks, nor of defining a wild will-to-power as *ultima ratio*[5] or arriving at an obscurely tragic and irrational conception of life.

Thus, in the first place it is necessary to become well aware that specifically warrior values, in the military context, are only representations of a reality which, in itself, can have a higher, not merely ethical, but even metaphysical meaning. Here we shall not repeat what we have already had the opportunity to discuss at

---

5   Latin: 'the last resort'.

length elsewhere:[6] we will only recall that ancient Aryan humanity habitually conceived of life as a perpetual battle between metaphysical powers, on the one hand the uranic forces of light and order, on the other hand the dark forces of chaos and matter. This battle, for the ancient Aryan, was fought and won both in the outer and in the inner world. And it was the exterior battle which reflected the battle to be fought in oneself, which was considered as the truly just war: the battle against those forces and peoples of the outer world which possessed the same character as the powers in our inner being which must be placed under subjection and domination until the accomplishment of a *pax triumphalis*.[7]

What follows from this is an interrelation of the true warrior-like or heroic ethos with a certain inner discipline and a certain superiority, an interrelation which, in one form or another, always appears in all our best traditions. That is why only one who is short-sighted or prejudiced can believe that the unavoidable consequence of putting forward a warrior-like vision of the world and of maintaining that the new Europe will have to be formed under the sign of the warrior spirit must be a chaos of unleashed forces and instincts. The true warrior ideal implies not only force and physical training but also a calm, controlled and conscious formation of the inner being and the personality. Love for distance and order, the ability to subordinate one's individualistic and passionate element to principles, the ability to place action and work above mere personhood, a feeling of dignity devoid of vanity are features of the true warrior spirit as essential as those

---

6   Cf. above all our work *Revolt Against the Modern World*, Hoepli, Milan 1934. (Note added by Evola.)

7   Even in the Christian doctrine of Saint Augustine, this view on the just war clearly remains: '*Proficientes autem nondumque perfecti ira* [to fight] *possunt, ut bonus quisque ex ea parte pugnet contra alterum, qua etiam contra semet ipsum; et in uno quippe homine caro concupiscit adversus spiritum et spiritus adversus carnem*' (*De Civ.*, XV, 5). ['But with the good, good men, or at least perfectly good men, cannot war; though, while only going on towards perfection, they war to this extent, that every good man resists others in those points in which he resists himself. And in each individual "the flesh lusts against the spirit, and the spirit against the flesh". From *St. Augustin's City of God and Christian Doctrine* (Grand Rapids: Eerdmans, 1988).] (Note added by Evola.)

which refer to actual combat: so that, from a higher point of view, combat itself can be worthwhile not so much for its immediate material results as for evidence of these qualities, which have a self-evident constructive value and can amount to elements of a special 'style', not only in a given area of the nation devoted specifically to soldiering, but also in a whole people and even beyond the frontiers of a given people.

This last point must be especially stressed, precisely in relation to our fight for a new Europe and a new European civilisation. The relation which, according to the aforementioned Aryan and traditional view, exists between inner struggle and 'just war' is useful, in addition, in preventing the equivocal irrationalism of a tragic and irrational vision of the world, and also allows one to go beyond a certain hardening, devoid of light, found in some subordinate aspects of the purely military style. According to the highest view, which is resurfacing today in the staunchest and most potent forces of our peoples, warrior-like discipline and combat are connected with a certain 'transfiguration' and participation in an effective 'spirituality'. This is how an idea of 'peace', which has nothing to do with the materialistic, democratic-bourgeois conception is outlined: it is a peace which is not the cessation of the spiritual tension at work in combat and in warrior-like asceticism, but rather a sort of calm and powerful fulfilment of it.

Fundamentally, it is here that the irreducible antithesis between the two different conceptions of 'civilisation' appears. There is not really 'imperialist materialism' and 'warlike brutality', on the one hand, and, on the other, 'love for culture' and interest in 'spiritual values'. Rather, there are spiritual values of a given type and of a properly Aryan origin, which oppose a different, intellectualistic, 'humanistic' and bourgeois conception of these. It is useless to delude ourselves that a warrior civilisation can have the same consideration for the so-called 'world of sciences and arts' as that which they enjoyed in the previous age of liberalism and of the Nineteenth-century bourgeoisie. They may retain their own significance but in a subordinate manner, because they represent not what is essential, but the accessory. The main thing consists instead in a certain inner style, a certain formation of the mind and character, a simplicity, clarity and harshness, a directly experienced meaning of existence, without expressionisms, without sentimentalisms, a pleasure for commanding, obeying, acting, conquering and overcoming oneself.

That the world of 'intellectuals' considers all this as 'unspiritual' and almost barbaric is natural, but it has no significance. A very different seriousness and depth from the point of view of which the 'culture' of the bourgeois world appears itself as a reign of worms, of forms without life and without force, belongs to the 'warrior' world. It will only be in a subsequent period when the new type of European is sufficiently formed that a new 'culture', less vain, less 'humanist', can be expected to reflect something of the new style.

Today it is very important to become aware of these aspects of the warrior spirit so that, in forming the bases of the future agreement and common civilisation of the European peoples, abstract and outdated ideas are not again brought into play. It is only by working from the energies which in the test of the fire of combat decide the freedom, dignity and mission of the peoples that true understanding, collaboration and unity of civilisation can be forged. And as these energies have little to do with 'culture' as understood by the 'intellectuals' and the 'humanists' to which they cannot be expected to rededicate themselves, so every abstract conception of right, all impersonal regulation of the relations between the various human groups and between the various States will appear intolerable to them. Here, another fundamental contribution which the warrior spirit can offer to the form and sense of a new European order becomes clear. Warrior spirit is characterised by direct, clear and loyal relations, based on fidelity and honour and a sound instinct for the various dignities, which it can well distinguish: it opposes everything which is impersonal and trivial. In every civilisation based on warrior spirit all order depends on these elements, not on legal paragraphs and abstract 'positivist' norms. And these are also the elements which can organise the forces, aroused by the experience of combat and consecrated by victory, into a new unity. That is why, in a certain sense, the type of warrior organisation which was peculiar to some aspects of the feudal Roman-Germanic civilisation can give us an idea of what, perhaps, will work, in an adapted form, for the new Europe for which today we fight. In dealing with relationships, not only man-to-man, but also State-to-State and race-to-race, it is necessary to be able to conceive again of that obedience which does not humiliate but exalts, that command or leadership which commits one to superiority and a precise responsibility. Instead of the legislation of an abstract 'international law' comprising peoples of any and all sorts, an organic right of European peoples based on these direct relationships must come about.

Suum cuique.[8] This Aryan and Roman principle defines the true concept of justice on the international plane as on the personal and is intimately connected to the warrior vision of life: everyone must have a precise sense of their natural and legitimate place in a well-articulated hierarchical whole, must feel pride in this place and adapt themselves to it perfectly. To this end, in fact, the 'ascetic' element also comprised in the warrior spirit will have a particular importance. To realise a new European order, various conditions are necessary: but there is no doubt that in the first place must be the 'asceticism' inherent in warrior discipline: the ability to see reality, suppressing every particularistic haughtiness, every irrational affection, every ephemeral pride; scorn for comfortable life and for all materialistic ideas of well-being; a style of simplicity, audacity and conscious force, in the common effort, on all planes.

---

8   Latin: 'to each his own'.

Varieties of Heroism[1]

A point to which we have often drawn the attention of our readers is that examination of the topic of 'inner race' is worthwhile, however incomplete it may remain at this stage, because of the fact that, rather than just noting the occurrence or non-occurrence of struggle and death among a people, it is necessary to consider their distinct 'style' and attitude regarding these phenomena and the distinct meanings which they may give to struggle and heroic sacrifice at any particular time. In fact, at least in general terms, we can speak of a scale along which individual nations may be placed according to how the value of human life is measured by them.

The vicissitudes of this war have exposed contrasts in this respect, which we would like to discuss briefly here. We shall limit ourselves essentially to the extreme cases, represented, respectively, by Russia and Japan.

Bolshevik Sub-Personhood

It is now well known that Soviet Russia's conduct of war does not attach the slightest importance to human life or to humanity as such. For them the combatants are nothing but 'human material' in the most brutal sense of this sinister expression – a sense which, unfortunately, has now become widespread in a certain

---

1   Originally published on 19 April 1942 as 'Volti dell'eroismo ' in 'Diorama mensile', *Il Regime Fascista*.

sort of military literature – a material to which no particular attention need be given and which, therefore, they need not hesitate to sacrifice in the most pitiless way, providing they have an adequate supply of it to hand. In general, as recent events have shown, the Russian can always face death readily because of a sort of innate, dark fatalism, and human life has been cheap for a long time in Russia. However, in the current use of the Russian soldier as the rawest 'human fodder' we see also a logical consequence of Bolshevik thought, which has the most radical contempt for all values derived from the idea of personhood and intends to free the individual from this idea, which it regards as superstition, and from the 'bourgeois prejudice' of the 'I' and the 'mine', in order to reduce him to the status of a mechanical member of a collective whole, which is the only thing which is regarded as important.

From these facts the possibility of a form of sacrifice and heroism which we would call 'telluric' and sub-personal, under the sign of the collective, omnipotent and faceless man, becomes apparent. The death of the bolshevised man on the battlefield represents, thus, the logical culmination of the process of depersonalisation, and of the destruction of every qualitative and personal value, which underlay the Bolshevik ideal of 'civilisation' all along. Here, what Erich Maria Remarque had tendentiously proposed in a book which became notorious as the comprehensive meaning of war can be accurately grasped: the tragic irrelevance of the individual in a situation where pure instinctuality, unleashed elemental forces and sub-personal impulses gain ascendancy over all conceivable values and ideals. Indeed, the tragic nature of this is not even felt, precisely because the sense of personhood has already vanished every higher horizon is precluded and collectivisation, even of the spiritual realm, has already struck deep roots in a new generation of fanatics, brought up on the words of Lenin and Stalin. We see here one specific form, albeit one almost incomprehensible to our European mentality, of readiness for death and self-sacrifice, which affords perhaps even a sinister joy in the destruction both of oneself and of others.

The Japanese Mysticism of Combat

Recent episodes of the Japanese war have made known to us a 'style' of dying which, from this point of view, seems to have affinities with that of Bolshevik man in that it appears to testify to the same contempt for the value of the individual and of personhood in general. Specifically, we have heard of Japanese airmen who, their planes loaded with bombs, hurl themselves deliberately upon their targets, and of soldiers who place mines and are doomed to die in their action, and it seems that a formal body of these 'volunteers for death' has been in existence in Japan for a long time. Once again, there is something in this which is hardly comprehensible to the Western mind. However, if we try to understand the most intimate aspects of this extreme form of heroism we find values which present a perfect antithesis to those of the lightless 'telluric heroism' of Bolshevik man.

The premises here are, in fact, of a rigorously religious or, to put it better, an ascetic and mystical character. We do not mean this in the most obvious and external sense – that is, as referring to the fact that in Japan the religious idea and the Imperial idea are one and the same thing, so that service to the Emperor is regarded as a form of divine service, and self-sacrifice for the *Tenno*[2] and the state has the same value as the sacrifice of a missionary or martyr – but in an absolutely active and combative sense. These are certainly aspects of the Japanese politico-religious idea: however, a more intimate explanation of the new phenomena must be looked for, on a higher plane than this, in the vision of the world and of life proper to Buddhism and above all to the Zen school, which has been rightly defined as the 'religion of the samurai', that is, of the Japanese warrior caste.

This 'vision of the world and of life' really strives to lift the possessor's sense of his own true identity to a transcendental plane, leaving to the individual and his earthly life a merely relative meaning and reality.

The first notable aspect of this is the feeling of 'coming from afar' – that is, that earthly life is only an episode, its beginning and

---

2   The Japanese term for the Emperor, meaning 'heavenly sovereign'.

ending are not themselves to be found here, it has remote causes, it is held in tension by a force which will express itself subsequently in other destinies, until supreme liberation. The second notable aspect, related to the first, is that the reality of the 'I' in simple human terms is denied. The term 'person' refers itself back to the meaning that it originally had in Latin, namely the mask of an actor, that is, a given way of appearing, a manifestation. Behind this, according to Zen, that is, the religion of the samurai, there is something incomprehensible and uncontrollable, infinite in itself and capable of infinite forms, so that it is called symbolically *sunya*, meaning 'empty', as against everything which is materially substantial and bound to specific form.

We see here the outline of the basis for a heroism which can be called 'supra-personal' – whereas the Bolshevik one was, contrarily, 'sub-personal'. One can take hold of one's own life and cast it away at its most intense moment out of super-abundance in the certainty of an eternal existence and of the indestructibility of what, never having had a beginning, cannot have an end. What may seem extreme to a certain Western mentality becomes natural, clear and obvious here. One cannot even speak here of tragedy – but for the opposite reason to that which applied in the case of Bolshevism: one cannot speak of tragedy because of the lived sense of the irrelevance of the individual in the light of the possession of a meaning and a force which, in life, goes beyond life. It is a heroism which we could almost call 'Olympian'.

And here, incidentally, we may remark on the dilettante triviality of one author who in a certain article has tried to demonstrate in four lines the pernicious character which such views, opposed to those which hold that earthly existence is unique and irrevocable, must have for the idea of the state and service to the state. Japan offers the most categorical refutation of such wild imaginings and the vigour with which our ally Japan wages her heroic and victorious battle demonstrates, on the contrary, the enormous warrior-like and spiritual potential which can proceed from the lived feeling of transcendence and supra-personhood to which we have referred.

Roman Devotio

Here it is appropriate to emphasise that, if the acknowledgment of the value of personhood is peculiar to the modern West, what is also peculiar to it is an almost superstitious emphasis on the importance of upbringing, which under recent conditions of democratisation has given rise to the famous concept of 'human rights' and to a series of socialistic, democratic and humanistic superstitions. Along with this clearly less than positive aspect there has been equal emphasis on the 'tragic', not to say 'Promethean', conception, which again represents a fall in level.

In opposition to all this we must recall the 'Olympian' ideals of our most ancient and purest traditions; we will then be able to conceive as equally ours an aristocratic heroism, free from passion, proper to beings whose life-centre is truly on a higher plane from which they are able to hurl themselves, beyond any tragedy, beyond any tie and any anguish, as irresistible forces.

Here, a little historical reminiscence is called for. Although this is not widely known, our ancient Roman traditions contained motifs concerning the disinterested, heroic offering of one's own person in the name of the state for the purpose of victory analogous to those which we have seen in the Japanese mysticism of combat. We are alluding to the so-called *devotio*. Its presuppositions are equally sacred. What acts in it is the general belief of the traditional man that invisible forces are at work behind the visible ones and that man, in his turn, can influence them.

According to the ancient Roman ritual of *devotio*, as we understand it, a warrior, and above all a chieftain, can facilitate victory by means of a mysterious unleashing of forces determined by the deliberate sacrifice of his own person, combined with the will not to come out of the fray alive. Let us recall the execution of this ritual by Consul Decius in the war against the Latins (340 BC),[3] and

---

3   Publius Decius Mus was a consul of the Roman Republic during the Latin War. He performed the *devotio* prior to the Battle of Vesuvius after an oracle predicted that he would not survive it. When the Roman attack began to falter, he called upon the gods to fulfil their promise and plunged single-handed into the army of the Latins and was killed. The Romans won the battle. His son of the same name also

also the repetition of it – exalted by Cicero[4] (*Fin.* II, 19, 61; *Tusc.* I, 37, 39) – by two other members of the same family. This ritual had its own precise ceremony, testifying to the perfect knowledge and lucidity of this heroic-sacrificial offer. In proper hierarchical order, first the Olympian divinities of the Roman state, Janus, Jupiter, Quirinus, and then, immediately following this, the god of war, Pater Mars, and then, finally, certain indigenous gods, were invoked: 'gods – it is said – which confer power to heroes over their enemies'; by the virtue of the sacrifice which these ancient Romans proposed to perform the gods were called upon to 'grant strength and victory to the Roman people, the Quirites, and effect the enemies of the Roman people, the Quirites, with terror, dismay, and death' (cf. Livy, 8:9).[5] Proposed by the pontifex,[6] the words of this formula were uttered by the warrior, arrayed in the *praetesta*, his foot upon a javelin. After that he plunged into the fray, to die. Incidentally, here the transformation of the sense of the word *devotio* must be noticed. While it applied originally to this order of ideas, that is, to a heroic, sacrificial and evocative action, in the later Empire it came to mean simply the fidelity of the citizen and his scrupulosness in making his payments to the state treasury (*devotio rei annonariae*). As Bouché-Leclercq[7] puts it, in the end, 'after Caesar was replaced by the Christian God, *devotio* means simply religiosity, the faith ready for all sacrifices, and then, in a further degeneration of the expression, devotion in the common sense of the word, that is, constant concern for salvation, affirmed in a meticulous and tremulous practice of the

---

performed the *devotio* during the Third Samnite War in 295 BC. His son in turn sacrificed himself in the Battle of Asculum in 279 BC.

4   Marcus Tullius Cicero (106 BC-43 BC) was a great Roman statesman and orator. Evola is likely referring to his works *De Finibus, Bonorum et Malorum* (*About the Ends of Goods and Evils*), and *Tusculanae Quaestiones* (*Questions Debated at Tusculum*).

5   Titus Livius (59 BC-17 AD), author of *The History of Rome*. This passage is taken from *Livy*, vol. 3 (London: A.J. Valpy, 1833), p. 16.

6   A pontifex was a priest in the ancient Roman religion.

7   Auguste Bouché-Leclercq (1842-1923), a French scholar of Roman history. His works have not been translated.

cult'. Leaving this aside, in the ancient Roman *devotio* we find, as we have shown, very precise signs of a mysticism aware of heroism and of sacrifice, binding the feeling of a supernatural and superhuman reality tightly to the will to struggle with dedication in the name of one's own chieftain, one's own state and one's own race. There are plenty of testimonies to an 'Olympian' feeling of combat and victory peculiar to our ancient traditions. We have discussed this extensively elsewhere. Let us only recall here that in the ceremony of the triumph, the victorious *dux*[8] displayed in Rome the insignia of the Olympian god to indicate the real force within him which had brought about his victory; let us recall also that beyond the mortal Caesar, Romanity worshipped Caesar as 'perennial victor', that is, as a sort of supra-personal force of Roman destiny.

Thus, if succeeding times have made other views prevail, the most ancient traditions still show us that the ideal of an Olympian 'heroism' has been our ideal as well, and that our people have also experienced the absolute offering, the consummation of their whole existence in a force hurled against the enemy in a gesture which justifies the most complete evocation of abysmal forces; and which brings about, finally, a victory which transforms the victors and enables their participation in supra-personal and 'fatal' powers. And so, in our heritage, points of reference are indicated which stand in radical opposition to the sub-personal and collectivist heroism we discussed above, and not only to that, but to every tragic and irrational vision which ignores what is stronger than fire and iron, and stronger than life and death.

---

8   Latin: 'leader'.

The Roman Conception of Victory[1]

Sallust described the original Romans as the most religious of mortals: *religiossimi mortales (Cat.,* 13),[2] and Cicero said that ancient Roman civilisation exceeded every other people or nation in its sense of the sacred: *omnes gentes nationisque superavimus (Hat: respon.,* IX, 19). Analogous testimonies are found in numerous variants in many other ancient writers. As against the prejudice of a certain historiography which persists in assessing ancient Rome from a solely legal and political point of view, what should be brought out is the fundamentally spiritual and sacred content of ancient Romanity, which should really be considered the most important element, because it is easy to show that the political, legal and ethical forms of Rome, in the last analysis, had as their common basis and origin precisely a special religious vision, a special type of relationship between man and the supra-sensory world.

But this relationship is of a quite different type from that characteristic of the beliefs which came to predominate subsequently. The Roman, like ancient and traditional men in general, believed in a meeting and mutual interpenetration of divine and human forces. This led him to develop a special sense of history and time, to which we have drawn attention in another of our articles here,

---

1   Originally published on 16 May 1943 as 'La concezione romana della Vittoria' in *Augustea*.

2   See note 4 in 'The Sacrality of War'.

speaking about a book by Franz Altheim.[3] The ancient Roman felt that the manifestation of the divine was to be found in time, in history, in everything which is carried out through human action, rather than in the space of pure contemplation, detached from the world, or in the motionless, silent symbols of a *hyperkosmia* or 'super-world'. He thus lived his history, from his very origins onwards, more or less in terms of 'sacred', or at the very least 'prophetic' history. In his *Life of Romulus* (1:8) Plutarch[4] says in so many words, 'Rome could not have acquired so much power if in one way or another it had not had a divine origin, such as to show to the eyes of men something great and inexplicable.'

Hence the typically Roman conception of an invisible and 'mystical' counterpart to everything visible and tangible which transpires in the human world. This is why rites accompanied every explanation of Roman life, whether individual, collective or political. Hence, also, the particular conception that the Roman had of fate: fate for him was not a blind power as it was for late ancient Greece, but the divine order of the world as development, to be interpreted and understood as means to an adequate science, so that the directions in which human action would be effective could be foretold, those along which this action could attract and actualise forces from above with a view not only to success, but also to a sort of transfiguration and higher justification.

Since this set of ideas applied to the whole of reality it reaffirmed itself also for ancient Rome in the field of warlike enterprises, of battle, heroism and victory. This fact allows us to see the error of those who consider the ancient Romans essentially as a race of semi-barbarians, who prevailed only through brutal force of arms, borrowing from other peoples, such as the Etruscans, Greeks and Syrians, the elements which served them in lieu of true culture. Rather, it is true that ancient Romanity had a particular mystical conception of war and victory, whose importance has oddly escaped the specialists in the study of Romanity, who have

3   Franz Altheim, *A History of Roman Religion* (London: Methuen & Co., 1938).

4   Mestrius Plutarchus (46-127) was a Greek historian. All of his biographies are collected in *Plutarch's Lives*.

limited themselves to pointing out the many and well-documented traditions in question in a distracted and inconsequential manner.

It was the essentially Roman opinion that, to be won materially, a war needed to be won – or, at least, favoured – mystically. After the Battle of Trasimene, Fabius says to the soldiers, 'Your fault is to have neglected the sacrifices and to have failed to heed the warnings of the oracles, rather than to have lacked courage or ability' (Livy, *History of Rome*, 17:9, cf. 31:5; 36:2; 42:2).

No Roman war began without sacrifices and a special college of priests – the Feciales – was in charge of the rituals related to war, which was considered a 'just war', *iustum bellum*, only after these had been performed. As once pointed out by de Coulanges,[5] the root of the military art of the Romans consisted originally in not being forced to fight when the gods were against it; that is, when by means of 'fatal' signs the agreement of forces from above with human forces was perceived to be absent.

Thus, the focus of the enterprise of war fell on a more than merely human plane – and both the sacrifice and the heroism of the combatant were considered to be more than merely human. The Roman conception of victory is particularly important.

In this conception every victory had a mystical side in the most objective sense of the term: in the victor, the chief, the imperator, applauded on the battlefield, was sensed the momentary manifestation of a divine force, which transfigured and trans-humanised him. The military victory ritual itself, in which the imperator (in the original sense, not of 'emperor', but of victorious chief) was lifted on a special shield, is not devoid of symbolism, as can be inferred from Ennius:[6] the shield, previously sanctified in the Capitoline temple of Jupiter, signifies here the *altisonum coeli clupeum*, the celestial sphere, beyond which victory raises the man who has won.

---

5   Numa Denis Fustel de Coulanges (1830-1889), a French historian. His principal work was *The Ancient City: A Study on the Religion, Laws, and Institutions of Greece and Rome*, Garden City: Doubleday, 1956.

6   Quintus Ennius (c. 239 BC-c. 169 BC) was a poet and historian of the Roman Republic. Only fragments of his works survive.

Revealing and unambiguous confirmations of this ancient
Roman conception are provided by the nature of the liturgy
and the pomp of the triumph. We speak of 'liturgy' since this
ceremony with which every winner was honoured had in Rome a
character much more religious than military. The victorious leader
appeared here as a sort of manifestation or visible incarnation of
the Olympian god, all the signs and the attributes of whom he
wore. The quadriga of white horses corresponded to that of the
solar god of the bright sky, and the mantle of the triumphant, the
purple toga embroidered with gold stars, reproduced the celestial
and stellar mantle of Jupiter. And so did the gold crown and the
sceptre which surmounted the Capitoline sanctuary. And the
winner dyed his face with minimum as in the cult of the temple
of the Olympian God, to which he then went to place solemnly
before the statue of Jupiter the triumphal laurels of his victory,
intending by this that Jupiter was its true author, and that he himself had gained it, essentially, as a divine force, a force of Jupiter:
hence the ritual identification in the ceremony.

The fact that the aforementioned cloak of the triumphant
corresponded to that of the ancient Roman kings could give rise
to further considerations: it could remind us of the fact brought
out by Altheim that even before the ceremony of the triumph
of the king was defined he had appeared in the primitive Roman
conception as an image of the celestial divinity: the divine order,
over which the latter presided, was reflected and manifested in
the human one, centred in the king. In this respect – in this conception, which, along with several others from the time of the
origins, was to resurface in the Imperial period – Rome testifies
to a universal symbolism, which is found again in a whole cycle
of great civilisations in the Indo-Aryan world and Aryo-Iranian
world, in ancient Greece, in ancient Egypt and in the Far East.

But, not to wander from the argument, let us point out another
characteristic element in the Roman conception of victory. It is
precisely because it was seen as a more than merely human event
that the victory of a chief often assumed for the Romans the
features of a *numen*, an independent divinity, whose mysterious

life was made the centre of a special system of rituals designed to feed it, enliven it and confirm its invisible presence among men. The most well-known example is provided by the *Victoria Caesaris*. Each victory was believed to actualise a new centre of forces, separate from the particular individuality of the mortal man who had realised it; or, if we prefer, by victory the victor had become a force existing in an almost transcendent order: a force not of the victory achieved in a given moment of history, but, as the Roman expression stated exactly, of a 'perpetual' or 'perennial' victory. The cult of such entities, established by law, was designed to stabilise, so to speak, the presence of this force, so that it added invisibly to those of the race, leading it towards outcomes of 'fortune', making of each new victory a means for revelation and reinforcement of the energy of the original victory. Thus, in Rome, since the celebration of the dead Caesar and that of his victory were one and the same, and the games, which had ritual meaning, were consecrated to the *Victoria Caesaris*, he could be considered as a 'perpetual victor'.

The cult of victory, which was believed to have prehistoric origins, can be said more generally to be the secret spirit of the greatness of Rome and of Rome's faith in its prophetic destiny. From the time of Augustus the statue of the goddess Victory had been placed on the altar of the Roman Senate, and it was customary that every senator, before taking office, went to this altar and burned a grain of incense. The force of victory seemed thus to preside invisibly over the deliberations of the *curia*;[7] hands reached out towards its image when, with the coming of a new Princeps,[8] fidelity was sworn to him and again on the Third of January of each year when solemn prayers were said in the Senate for the health of the Emperor and the prosperity of the Empire. It is particularly worthy of interest that this was the most tenacious Roman cult of so-called 'paganism', surviving after the destruction of all the others.

---

7 The Roman Senate.

8 Another term for the Roman Emperor.

Other considerations could be derived from the Roman notion of *mors triumphalis*, 'triumphal death', which shows various aspects with which we will perhaps deal on another occasion. Here we just want to add something about one special aspect of the heroic dedication connected to the ancient Roman concept of *devotio*. It expresses what in modern terms could be called a 'tragic heroism', but linked to a sense of supra-sensory forces and a higher and very specific purpose.

In ancient Rome *devotio* did not mean 'devotion' in the modern sense of the meticulous and over-scrupulous practice of a religious cult. It was, rather, a warlike ritual action in which the sacrifice of oneself was vowed and one's own life was dedicated consciously to 'lower' powers, whose unleashing was to contribute to bringing victory, on one the hand, by endowing one with irresistible strength and, on the other hand, by causing panic to the enemy. It was a rite established formally by the Roman State as a supernatural addition to arms in desperate cases, when it was believed that the enemy could hardly be defeated by normal forces.

From Livy (8:9) we know all the details of this tragic ritual and also the solemn formula of evocation and self-dedication which the one who intended to sacrifice himself for victory had to pronounce, repeating it from the pontifex, clothed in the *praetesta*, his head veiled, his hand at his chin and his foot on a javelin. After that he plunged to his death in the fray, a hurled, 'fatal' force, no longer human. There were noble Roman families in which this tragic ritual was almost a tradition: for example, three of the stock of the Deci performed it in 340 B.C. in the war against the rebellious Latins, then again in 295 in the war against the Samnites, and once more in 79 at the Battle of Ascoli: as if this was 'a family law', as Livy puts it.

As pure inner attitude this sacrifice may recall, by its perfect lucidity and its voluntary character, what still happens today in Japan's war: we have heard of special torpedo boats, or of Japanese aeroplanes, hurled with their crew against the target and, once again, the sacrifice, almost always performed by members of the ancient warrior aristocracy, the samurai, has a ritual and mystical aspect. The difference is certainly that they do not aim at a more than merely material action, a true evocation, to the same extent as in the ancient Roman theory of the *devotio*.

And naturally, the modern and, above all, Western atmosphere for thousands of reasons which have become, so to speak, constitutive of our being over the centuries makes it extremely difficult to feel and to move forces behind the scenes and to give every gesture, every sacrifice, every victory, transfiguring meanings, such as those discussed above. It is however certain that, even today, in this unleashed vicissitude one should not feel alone on the battlefields – one should sense, in spite of everything, relationships with a more than merely human order, and paths which cannot be assessed solely by the values of this visible reality can be the source of a force and an indomitability whose effects on any plane, in our view, should not be underestimated.

Liberations[1]

It is a principle of ancient wisdom that situations as such never matter as much as the attitude that is assumed while in them, and therefore the meaning that is attributed to them. Christianity, generalising from a similar viewpoint, has been able to speak of life as of a 'test' and has adopted the maxim *vita est militia super terram*.

In the quiet and ordered periods of history, this wisdom is accessible only to a few chosen ones, since there are too many occasions to surrender and to sink, to consider the ephemeral to be the important, or to forget the instability and contingency which is the natural state of things. It is on this basis that what can be called, in the broader sense, the mentality of bourgeois life is organised: it is a life which does not know either heights or depths, and develops interests, affections, desires and passions which, however important they may be from the merely earthly point of view, become petty and relative from the supra-individual and spiritual point of view, which must always be regarded as proper to any human existence worthy of the name.

The tragic and disrupted periods of history ensure, by force of circumstances, that a greater number of persons are led towards an awakening, towards liberation. And really and essentially it is by this that the deepest vitality of a stock, its virility and its unshakability, in the superior sense, can be measured. And today

---

1   Originally published on 3 November 1943 as 'Liberazioni' in *La Stampa*.

in Italy on that front which by now no longer knows any distinction between combatants and non-combatants, and has therefore seen so many tragic consequences, one should get used to looking at things from this higher perspective to a much greater extent than is usually possible or necessary.

From one day to the next, even from one hour to the next, as a result of a bombing raid one can lose one's home and everything one most loved, everything to which one had become most attached, the objects of one's deepest affections. Human existence becomes relative – it is a tragic and cruel feeling, but it can also be the principle of a catharsis and the means of bringing to light the only thing which can never be undermined and which can never be destroyed. We need to remember that, for a complex set of reasons, the superstition which attaches all value to purely individual and earthly human life has spread and rooted itself tenaciously – a superstition which, in other civilisations, was and remains almost unknown. The fact that, nominally, the West professes Christianity has had only a minimal influence in this respect: the whole doctrine of the supernatural existence of the spirit and of its survival beyond this world has not undermined this superstition in any significant way; it has not caused knowledge of what did not begin with birth and cannot end with death to be applied in the daily, sentimental and biological life of a sufficient number of beings. Rather, people have clung convulsively to that small part of the whole which is the short period of this existence of individuals, and have made every effort to ignore the fact that the hold on reality afforded by individual life is no firmer than that of a tuft of grass which one might grab to save himself from being carried away by a wild current.

It arouses this awareness precisely not as something cerebral or 'devotional', but rather as a living fact and liberating feeling, which everything today that is tragic and destructive can have, at least for the best of us: creative value. We are not recommending insensitivity or some misconceived stoicism. Far from it: it is a matter of acquiring and developing a sense of detachment towards oneself, towards things and towards persons, which should instil a calm, an incomparable certainty and even, as we have before stated, an indomitability. It is like simplifying oneself, divesting oneself in a state of waiting, with a firm, whole mind, and with an awareness of something which exists beyond all existence. From this state the capacity will also be found of always being able to begin again, as if *ex nihilo*,[2] with a new and fresh mind, forgetting what has been and what has been lost, focusing only on what positively and creatively can still be done.

A radical destruction of the 'bourgeois' who exists in every man is possible in these disrupted times more than in any other. In these times man can find himself again, can really stand in front of himself and get used to watching everything according to the view from the other shore, so as to restore to importance, to essential significance, what should be so in any normal existence: the relationship between life and the 'more than life', between the human and the eternal, between the short-lived and the incorruptible.

And to find ways over and above mere assertion and gimmickry, for these values to be positively lived, and to find forceful expression in the greatest possible number of persons in these hours of trial is undoubtedly one of the main tasks facing the politico-spiritual elite of our nation.

---

2   Latin: 'out of nothing'.

The Decline of Heroism[1]

War and rearmament in the world of the 'Westerners' is once again about guaranteeing security. Intensive propaganda with a crusading tone, using all its tried and tested methods, is in the air. Here, we cannot go thoroughly into the concrete questions which concern our specific interests, but rather hint at something more general, one of the inner contradictions of the notion of war, which undermines the foundations of the so-called 'West'.

The technocratic error of thinking of 'war potential' primarily in terms of arms and armaments, special technical-industrial equipment and the like, and assessing man – according to the brutal expression now widespread in military literature – simply as 'human resources' – has already been widely criticised. The quality and spirit of the men to whom the arms, the means of offence and destruction, are given have represented, still represent and will always represent the basic element of 'war potential'. No mobilisation will ever be 'total' if men whose spirit and vocation are up to the tests which they must face cannot be created.

How are things, in this respect, in the world of the 'democracies'? They now want, for the third time in this century, to lead humanity to war in the name of 'the war against war'. This requires men to fight at the same time that war as such is criticised. It demands heroes while proclaiming pacifism as the highest ideal.

---

1   Originally published on 1 October 1950 as 'Tramonto degli eroi ' in *Meridiano d'Italia*.

It demands warriors while it has made 'warrior' a synonym for attacker and criminal, since it has reduced the moral basis of 'the just war' to that of a large-scale police operation, and it has reduced the meaning of the spirit of combat to that of having to defend oneself as a last resort.

The Bourgeois Ideal

Let us examine this problem more closely. In what cause should the man of 'the Western bloc' go to war and face death? It is obviously nonsensical to respond in the name of the bourgeois ideal, the carefully maintained 'security' of existence which abhors risk, which promises that the maximum comfort of the human animal shall be easily accessible to all. Few will be deluded enough to imagine that, by sacrificing themselves, they can secure all this for future generations. Some will try to make others go and fight instead of them, offering as inducements beautiful words about humanitarianism, glory and patriotism. Apart from this, the only thing a man in such a world will fight for is his own skin.

His skin is the same in Curzio Malaparte's[2] sense as here: 'Certainly, only the skin is undeniable and tangible. One no longer fights for honour, for freedom, for justice. One fights for this disgusting skin. You cannot even imagine what man is capable of, of what heroisms and infamies, to save his skin.'

If one wants a profession of faith from the democratic world beyond all its pretences, it is contained in these words. They express the only credo, leaving aside mere verbiage and lies, with which it can spiritually equip its army. This means to rush to the crusade against the Communist threat only out of physical terror; of terror for one's own skin; for the frightening, wavering ideal of

---

2   Curzio Malaparte (1898-1957) was an Italian writer and journalist. Originally a Fascist supporter, he turned against Fascism after covering the war on the Eastern front for the Italian newspapers (documented in his books *Kaputt* and *The Volga Rises in Europe*). Here, Evola is referring to his post-war novel about the struggles of life in Italy under Allied occupation, *The Skin* (Evanston: Northwestern University Press, 1997).

Babbitt;[3] of bourgeois safety; of the 'civilisation' of the domesticated and standardised human animal, which eats and copulates, and the limits of whose horizon is *Reader's Digest*, Hollywood and the sports stadiums.

Thus, those who are fundamentally lacking in heroism will seek to awaken warriors for the 'defence of the West' by playing upon the complex of anxiety. Since they have deeply demoralised the true Western soul; since they have debased and demeaned, firstly, the true basis of the state, hierarchy and virile solidarity; and secondly, the notion of war and combat, they must now play the 'trump card' of the anti-Bolshevik crusade.

Enough of Illusions

Not many illusions can remain concerning the sort of 'morality' which can support this endeavour and which no industrial mobilisation with atomic bombs, flying superfortresses, supersonic fighters and so on, can replace. It is with these 'trump cards' alone that the 'Western world' now stands on the threshold of a possible third worldwide cataclysm, having broken down and insulted everything which had survived from the authentic warrior traditions of Europe and the Far East.

In the opposing bloc there are forces which combine technology with the elemental force of fanaticism, of dark and savage determination and of the contempt for individual life found among masses which, whether through their own ancient traditions or through the exaltation of the collectivist ideology, hardly value their own existence. This is the tide which will swell forth not only from the Red East, but from the whole of a contaminated and unleashed Asia.

However, what is really required to defend 'the West' against the sudden rise of these barbaric and elemental forces is the strengthening, to an extent perhaps still unknown to Western

---

3   *Babbitt* is a novel first published in 1922 by the American writer Sinclair Lewis (New York: Harcourt, Brace & Co.). As a result of its popularity, the term 'Babbitt' became synonymous with bourgeois conformism and philistinism, which is the theme of the novel.

man, of a heroic vision of life. Apart from the military-technical apparatus, the world of the 'Westerners' has at its disposal only a limp and shapeless substance – and the cult of the skin, the myth of 'safety' and of 'war on war', and the ideal of the long, comfortable, guaranteed, 'democratic' existence, which is preferred to the ideal of the fulfilment which can be grasped only on the frontiers between life and death in the meeting of the essence of living with the extreme of danger.

Some will object that after all that Europe has been through, we have had enough of 'militarism' and war-mongering, and 'total war' should be left in the past and forgotten. Granted, 'militarism' can be left behind us since it is only a degraded, inferior echo of a heroic (and far from exclusively belligerent) conception, and to condemn all heroism as 'militarism' is one of the expedients of 'democratic' propaganda, an expedient which has now begun to backfire on its proponents. In any case, unfortunately there probably won't be any choice. It will be hard for the forces already in motion to stop (in general, irrespective of the outcome of the current Korean affair) and there will only remain one course of action: to ride the tiger,[4] as the Hindu expression puts it.

One of the most highly praised contemporary writers in Europe has written things about modern war which he experienced thoroughly and actively (he volunteered, was injured eighteen times, and was awarded the highest German military decoration), whose value will become more and more obvious in the times to come.[5] He has said that modern man, by creating the world of technology and putting it to work, has signed his name to a debt which he is now required to pay. Technology, his creature, turns against him, reduces him to its own instrument

---

4 An expression frequently used by Evola, particularly in his book of the same name, to describe the problems faced by an individual who attempts to resist the norms and values of the modern world while simultaneously being forced to live in it.

5 Evola is referring to the German writer Ernst Jünger (1895-1998), and specifically his 1932 work *Der Arbeiter* (*The Worker*), which has not been translated into English. However, many of the ideas from *Der Arbeiter* are summarised in Jünger's own essay 'Total Mobilisation', which is available in English in Richard Wolin (ed.), *The Heidegger Controversy* (New York: Columbia University Press, 1991).

and threatens him with destruction. This fact manifests itself most clearly in modern war: total, elemental war, the merciless struggle with materiality itself. Man has no choice but to confront this force, to render himself fit to answer this challenge, to find in himself hitherto unsuspected spiritual dimensions, to awake to forms of extreme, essentialised, heroism, forms which, while caring nothing for his person, nevertheless actualise what the aforementioned author calls the 'absolute person' within him, thus justifying the whole experience.

There is nothing else one can say. Perhaps this challenge will constitute the positive side of the game for especially qualified men, given that game must be accepted and played out anyway. The preponderance of the negative part, of pure destruction, may be frightening, infernal. But no other choice is given to modern man since he himself is the sole author of the destiny and the aspect which he is now starting to see.

This is not the moment to dwell on such prospects. Besides, what we have said does not concern any nation in particular, nor even the present time. It concerns the time when things will become serious, globally, not merely for the interests of the bourgeois, capitalist world, but for those men who know and, at that point, will still be able to gather together into an unshakeable bloc.

Index

Other books published by Arktos:

Why We Fight
by Guillaume Faye

De Naturae Natura
by Alexander Jacob

It Cannot Be Stormed
by Ernst von Salomon

The Saga of the Aryan Race
by Porus Homi Havewala

Against Democracy and Equality: The European New Right
by Tomislav Sunic

The Problem of Democracy
by Alain de Benoist

The Jedi in the Lotus
by Steven J. Rosen

Archeofuturism
by Guillaume Faye

A Handbook of Traditional Living

Tradition & Revolution
by Troy Southgate

Can Life Prevail?
A Revolutionary Approach to the Environmental Crisis
by Pentti Linkola

Metaphysics of War:
Battle, Victory & Death in the World of Tradition
by Julius Evola

The Path of Cinnabar:
An Intellectual Autobiography
by Julius Evola

Journals published by Arktos:

The Initiate: Journal of Traditional Studies

CPSIA information can be obtained
at www.ICGtesting.com
Printed in the USA
LVHW030738011218
598839LV00003B/144/P